REFLECTIONS is a non-profit making arts project which believes that art in its various forms, can provide a suitable forum for like-minded individuals to share their ideas in a positive environment. Now, perhaps more than ever, there is a need for goodwill between people, irrespective of their background, social position, or standing. The purpose of 'Reflections' therefore, is to promote this aim rather than be a platform for self-interested personalities.

This selection by Alan Jacobs, Editor of the Element Book of Mystical Verse.

P.O.BOX 178, SUNDERLAND, SR1 1DU

REFLECTIONS

AN ANTHOLOGY OF
CONTEMPORARY
MYSTICAL
VERSE

COMPILED
WITH AN INTRODUCTION BY
ALAN JACOBS

ROWAN PRESS

This edition first published in 2000 by
ROWAN PRESS
PO BOX 32
DARLINGTON
CO. DURHAM
DL1 5YY
ENGLAND

Printed and bound in Great Britain by
SRP Limited
Exeter EX2 7LW

ISBN   1 874309 02 7

The Poet's Task

To hold the pen again, but now inspired
By images which form before the eyes,
By stories, themes, ideas, that gather strength,
All crying for conversion into words.

To zealously transcribe those radiant thoughts,
As though a flow of deep emotive force
Is being guided by a master's brush
To animate his picture of the world.

To move from place to place across the globe
In search of something yet to be defined,
But taking note of strange, heroic tales
Which still survive in these enlightened days.

To roam at will across forgotten realms,
Long-lost before our calendar began,
And from the broken structures that remain
To re-create the grandeur that has gone.

To illustrate the irony of man,
In words that sweep across the worldwide stage,
To show his tragic conflict with himself -
Against a background of relentless time.

To reach within the reader's mind and paint
Enchanted visions that will spring to life,
With messages of subtlety and depth,
To stir those passions dormant in his heart.

Sidney Morleigh

CONTENTS

INTRODUCTION

Like most of the very best in this miraculous life, true gold is both hard to find and hard to mine. 'Reflections' is offered mainly to its subscribers and is not widely known by the general educated-public interested in what Shelley called 'Higher Poetry'. As he wrote in his magnificent essay 'A Defence of Poetry'

> "A great poem is a fountain forever overflowing with the waters of wisdom and delight".

The philosophy of Reflections is 'egolessness' and she does not wish to be a platform for self-interested personalities. All Higher Poetry, which is mystical in character comes from vision after the diminution, if not the abnegation of the petty obsessive self; so that the intuitions of the Real Self may flow through the poet's trained mental equipment. The Editorial Board remain anonymous and so demonstrate this principle in action.

Mystical Poetry is an expression of the Soul's yearning to be reunited with her Source. Reflections' Poets follow the mainstream of classical English prosody, honouring structure, metre, quantity and often rhyme. This selection from nine years of successful publication is broadly chronological, and chosen to be representative of her poets' work.

She is a happy counterbalance and antidote to much of the contemporary verse which deals with more mundane subject matter not generally to the public's liking. Reflections' Poets are musical - and sing!

Reflections is indeed an oasis in the desert of overworked free verse often indistinguishable from prose except for line breaks. Let all those who yearn for living waters, slake their thirst in her fountains and return; renewed and refreshed.

Alan Jacobs
London, April 2000

Prayer To A New-born Child

Come out sacred womb-child,
Enter into the lightning-dance of life.
Don't be afraid of life in its flashing madness,
Don't be afraid to endure the bitter realms of doubt and darkness.
Look in blind wonder towards the majestic sun, piercing deep
                              through skies of strife.
We are all dreamers, shining souls in mountain heights,
We are all searching for the heart of light,
We all dream of flower kingdoms and radiant sights,
We are all spirits of gravity, longing to rise to phoenix heights.

Autumn

Once again the year turns its key in the lock of my Self
And gummed pine-incense, drifting in still, white mists
Turns my mind inwards to the voice that tells no lies.
Here I stand again, looking to the distant, laughing Spring,
One world dying, another not yet inspired by the spark-filled Word.
O come Light, Come, and make mockery of Winter's testy grip
Come, enter the cave and cast your sparkling spells.
The seeds are long sown and await the rites of Spring.
Come Light, Come, and stir the sleeping waters
That fire-green Truth might germinate, and push
Its countless shoots down into a world made ready.
O come and laugh in the face of seeming pain,
Come, and joke amid the phantom burdens, the trials and the tears,
For what are they at best but the lackeys of the Coming Dawn?

Behest

Send down the power magic man,
Seek out my own pure heart.
Gross is subtle; lead is gold,
To me your light impart.

I have ready a God-given task
That none save we may see.
Send down the power magic man
And partners we shall be.

Protection there is plenty now,
For nought can damage Peace,
And rumbling echoes here below
At my bidding always cease.

So send down the power magic man
And give me please my test.
I reckon I am ready now
And know what I request.

Rebirth

The flower smiles a fragrance,
The man laughs a reply,
And the air smooths the rippling waters
Of a scattered Earth.
And I understand the mountains,
And the whisperings of the Oak.
The sun melts golden,
Onto the fountain rose.
And I am alive
And I am the sun
And I am the rose.

Purpose

The seeds lay ripening beneath the land, unseen, unheard as if in
                                                                dreams,
And so are we, enclothed in flesh, amassed in roots but lacking shoots,
Come, Awake! the summer rains are here.

O summer days and truthful rains, ease the burden below the main,
Lift we seeds and let us stand, with gladness rejoice the Farmer's hand,
Hear our prayer Lord, hear our prayer.

Growing goodness fills the fields, waves of young-corn greet the sky,
Man! Lift up thy shoot to hidden sun, whose inner secrets ye know
                                                                none
Lift up I say and greet the Dawn.

The golden corn in splendour looking up has left the soil, has won
Now hark! the Herald Angels sing, be thou reaped thy first work done,
And feel the cries of many.

Now corn of God and bread of light, go feed the hungry souls
Who lacking strength to rend the veil, turn to darker ways and pain
My Son, go give your Life and Light and Love. Amen.

The Autumn Rose

You are The Rose
That was born of the Autumn sun.
That brooding, smould'ring orb
That fleets its failing rays:
Down through the dense, moist evergreen
Of the pine forest.
A season's last light
Will struggle; and die in cold flame:
On the serpentine, needle-strewn paths
That lead to everywhere.....
And to nowhere!

You are The Rose
That will thrive beside the choked fountain:
Whose leaf smother'd basin
Stares up at the fast-dark'ning skies.
A lone bird cries;
And so heralds the onset of Winter.
Willowherb skeletons
Reach up to grasp at dank nothingness:
Cock-Pheasant preen;
And strut through undergrowth

You are The Rose
That blows alongside the wild orchid:
That tangles and twines
With the bramble, broom and bracken.
Soft, fresh breezes
Caress your pale petals

Yet, you are The Rose
That will transcend all seasons:

For you are The Rose.

The Autumn Rose!

Before The Birth

Like warm Christmas candles on a winter's night,
The fiery stars glittered and magically blazed,
And in the deep frosty sky, the Music of the Spheres
Spread their message symphonic to the silent Earth;
Jack Frost with his icy brush the windows dressed,
And hung with gem stone lanterns the frozen doors,
The Queen of the North, draped in blue-silvered robes,
Passed like a whisper on shivering wings,
And brushed with her misty fingers the tinkling icicles,
Her song strangely hidden in the cold, moaning winds,
As she veiled the sleepy world with her snow-white sheets;
Meanwhile, tears like hot jewels did sadly fall
From beauteous eyes, once filled with honey-dew and fire,
And froze there...still...like granite-glass stones,
Gripping the velvet cheeks with sorrow's freezing hand,
Imprisoning within its ice-stone wall, the warm flame of Love.
Not yet would the humble snowdrops and crocus flames
Dare their innocent heads above the bitter snows,
Nor yet would the laughing daffodils, dressed in Solar Gold,
Dare to imitate the Sun of our Love,
While rules that Queen of the Wintery North.

Harvest Festival

In the morning of the new day
there arrived mysteriously on earth
men with ancient golden hearts.

Like great, immovable trees
they were planted.
Not one of the elements could injure them
for their roots were set deep
and their trunks were ample and straight.
And their uppermost branches swayed gently
in the spiritual breezes of heaven.

I wonder if, when the mists clear,
we'll circle them, weaving long-forgotten patterns,
dancing and chanting holy chants,
and fill again our empty baskets with windfall fruit.

A Gift

I will kiss with Love your tear-stained cheeks,
And softly Light your eyes with Spirit Flames,
I will stir with Joy your poor, broken Heart,
And fill with Vital Power your sluggish veins,
I will with blessed Radiance feed thy Sight,
And with Charmed Melodies hymn the passing hours,
I will fill you up full with the Strength of Peace,
And make you Simple like the meadow flowers.

As The Butterfly

As the Butterfly weaved
Her frail journey through hedgerows:
Past flowers and grasses
That would grow by her way.
As the Butterfly loved;
Lived to bring understanding:
Left behind her the promise
Of some perfect day.

As the Butterfly danced
Upon soft, perfumed breezes
That brushed the fresh meadows;
Swayed the unripened corn.
As the Butterfly cherished
Each moment of summer;
Then was plucked from Life's pathway:
Her soul was reborn.

She, as one now with Nature;
Whose relentless rhythm:
The Rhythm of Spirit
That beats ever on.
So shall her soul shine
Through dark winters that follow:
She will float on forever
'Cross the fields far beyond.

Winter

The tangled life of Autumn does end
And winter sets sail to come from afar,
Trailing its cloak of misery and gloom,
Bringing great portents of death and of doom.

The King of the North creeps out of his den
Brightening the hearts of children and men!
Why? - Not for the cold and the rain that it brings,
But for cradling Christmas, with the carols we sing.

O, life that does in Winter die
Where is your charm?
Can anyone find
That sweet, soft, simple healing balm?

That balm which outstrips all the misery and gloom
And sets children's hearts alight with a new fuel.
For the blanket descends and silence prevails,
Except for the merry, muffled sound of snow games.

Now all is silent, now all is still,
And the white life abounding that gave us a thrill
Is dead, gaunt, forgotten, forlorn and in pain;
Crying for mercy, but dispersed by the rain.

For Winter is ended and death is all gone,
Supplanted by Springtime with fragrances strong.
And life may return, and flowers may bend,
Till the tangled life of Autumn does surely end.

Calm Centre

Sometimes upon life's road,
When all seems dark and the struggle hard,
Then comes sweet Peace,
To lead us back to that simple state,
Where the soft radiance of Heaven calms the troubled mind,
Revealing how, in the heated frenzy of the Game,
True Living has passed us by.

How then our complex lives are simplified,
And filled with summer Goodness,
Flowing like a calm harmonic stream,
In all directions from the Heart's rich Core,
And we are stilled; within our rightful Place,
Viewing all surrounding troubles with a calm composure,
In the Beauty of our Central Standing Ground.

How comes it then, that we so swiftly lose that state,
And filled with bitter cares bemoan our lives?
How comes it then, that we quickly grasp at all commotion,
And bewildered jump from hour to hour?
One fleeting moment is all it takes
For the lower powers to grasp the reins,
And draw their dismal clouds across the Sun!

Therefore, be ever Watchful from your little Golden Seat,
And see how every mood is like the horse's hooves;
Get not involved in pushing and pulling,
As you travel life's mysterious highway,
But Rule the fiery steeds with the grip of joy;
Then will you calmly sit in Bright Perception,
Like a precious Diamond in Eternal Light.
A Guiding Star to your Brothers and Sisters!

Towards The Golden Fleece

I

Perseus slew Medusa, wielding Athene's mirror shield of wisdom,
to see that head of viprous tresses
lest he be turned to stone.

Suffering writhing snakes in my own being; impartially,
silently witnessing, I gaze within.

A cool clear long impersonal reflective look
freezes my Gorgon too, stone-dead
for a time.

II

Narcissus condemned by Nemesis to succumb to his beauty
reflected in a pool;
futile passion held him in grip
he wasted away.

As a toddler I climbed up to a mirror
spied a stranger
touched skin
so did the other
I kissed his glassy lips

Now after loosening the grip
that's stuck me to that thing out there ever decaying
I occasionally catch odd glimpses of my original face.

III

Atlas, father of the stars held up heaven on his shoulders
relieved once, for a while, by Heracles.
Sometimes I feel like Atlas carrying the world-burden on my back.

I see his statue straining to hold up a globe
when his feet are firmly rooted in the creative ground of existence,

I am temporarily relieved by this Heraclean thought.

IV

Heracles' labour was to clean King Augeias's filthy stables
In one day he succeeded by diverting a river through the yard.

Sometimes I feel my mind needs cleansing.

Perhaps by bathing in a love-current I can restore my land to health
without soiling so much as a little finger like Heracles.

Real brain-washing in a pure thought stream.

V

Eos, dawn Goddess, married mortal Tithonus
forgetting to ask almighty Zeus to grant him eternal youth
as well as immortality.

Because of this mountainous Olympic error he aged endlessly
until when dessicated was incarcerated
changed into a cicada to chirp his ratchety treble ad infinitum

Instead of being over involved in the world
It may have been wiser if I had stayed a blushing maiden
Pursued forever by my lover the Sun of pure consciousness?

VI

Pandora first mortal woman whom Zeus created
from clay and Athene gave the breath of life:
foolish mischievous idle but beautiful
married Epimetheus 'he who thinks afterwards'

His brother Prometheus 'he who thinks before' warned them never to
open her jar
in which were imprisoned all spites
Pandora, over curious, disobeyed, and out swarmed clouds of vicious
flies

Prometheus had also enjarred Hope so saving them from suicide

Now when I let out inadvertently
any of Pandora's insects in myself
injecting venom into my space
anger fear malice envy ad nauseam,
there is still the Promethean Hope
to wait patiently, for poison clears in time

Meanwhile if I feel any of these noxious
winged beasties buzzing around
I either swat them hard
dissolve them in a solution of awareness
welcome them in the Hope they will be transmuted
or avoid them like the Black Death.

VII

Daedalus a supersmith was instructed
in his art by Goddess Athene:
locked up in a labyrinth by King Minos
with his enslaved son Icarus,
he escaped to fashion wings for them both
but ran out of thread
only large quills were sewn,
small feathers stuck by wax.

"My son be warned! never soar too high
lest the sun melts the wax, nor swoop too low
follow me closely, do not set your own course
lest your feathers be wetted by the sea."

Icarus disobeyed, rejoiced by the lift of his great wings
he soared to the sun, Apollo melted the wax, he drowned.

Now when I try flying to the Sun in myself
get out of control and fall,
and losing my thread of attention, wax wayward with untried notions,
I remember that Daedalus, the master craftsman
who cared for every detail, survived,
and zoom in again.

VIII

Pluto rules Hades, a dominion close to the pool of Lethe
where the ghosts never know what is happening in the world,
let alone in Olympus,
except for the fragments which come
when they wail in suffering:
his most prized possession is his cap of invisibility.

Sometimes when collapsing into lethargy
I remember the still waters of Asphodel's meadows
and think that if this kingdom of sHades is so beautiful
is it because it is lit by the Sun of Elysium, pure awareness?

I think I would prefer dwelling in Asphodel
close to the pool of recollection,
but better still in Elysium,
a happy land of perpetual day where, among other joys, Helen and
                                                              Achilles
hold high revelry and declaim Homeric rhapsodies.

To get near there and find out
Rhadamantine Judges have to decide
whether you have practised a trait now obsolete called 'Vertue'

the prime meaning of this archaism
is the power inherent in a divine being

quite a work
anyway there's no harm in trying now and again
before old Charon comes to ferry me across the Styx.

IX

Orpheus famed poet and musician
his lyre a gift from Apollo,
the phrases 'Know thyself!' and 'Nothing in excess' always on his lips,
taught by the Muses; enchanted wild beasts made even trees and rocks
to dance,
saved the Argo by countering the ravishing but deadly
Siren's chorus with celestial music of the spheres:
married Eurydice who carelessly stepped on a snake and died.
Vowing to rescue her from the underworld
his skill charmed Charon, the ferryman,
the many-headed guard dog Cerberus and the Stern Judges of the Dead;
he soothed the tortures of the damned and swayed the savage heart of
Hades
who let him guide her back through the darkness of Erebus by his
sublime lyrics;
but only if he never looked back until reaching daylight.
He turned too early to see if she was there and lost her.

Sometimes listening to a golden strain of sweet harmonic melody
which opens up my heart to love
my strumpet mind mischievously wanders back to a sad memory
and I lose my beloved with an agonising jolt.

I wish I could follow Hades's advice and never look back
Until I reach the Sun's full splendour and bathe in its light.

X

Jason hero of heroes sought the Golden Fleece
That which had the power to end all sorrow
after building a sound ship, training a cunning crew
he sailed for ancient Colchis to the edge of the known world

guided by his divine protectress Hera,
surmounting titanic obstacles he eventually won through.

After netting my furious Harpies
loathsome creatures whom at every meal fly into the palace and snatch
the victuals
avoiding the Symplegades
clashing rocks of angry yea and nay
and slaying dear Telos my brazen egotistic monster
I catch sight of that sacred Fleece
whose touch transforms soul's iron to gold
hidden at the voyage's end.

A glimpse is worth this Argosy;
such healing lustrous bliss!

Freeing

By deep pool am I enchanted
Held fast, steady, to this magnet

By still grove is my heart captive
Bound in silence everlasting

By skylark song am I seduced
From heavens high, to earth reduced

By daisy lawn is my mind lost
In making chains beyond all cost

By gummed pine scent, am I drawn in
Never to be set free again

By Desire
Am I chained to these
The like of which are, simply,
Keys.

Free Spirit

Oh - to be free
Free to fly
To glide
To soar
To rise, with ease
Above
To spread my wings
And go
To leave behind
My burdens and cares
To know
Freedom
No limitations, no chains
Free to be myself
To be
Whole.

Adam's Dream

I

Poor modern Adam, so sadly forlorn,
The tread-mill of life has torn down his soul;
Sometimes he wishes he'd never been born
And yearns for a way to make himself Whole.

Like a traveller lost in a bleak desert place
And blinded by sense-storms with savourless food,
He calls for water crying out for grace,
He prays to discover the source of the Good.

Entrapped like a bee on a jammed window pane
He drones up and down, in search of the light,
Until tumbling exhausted, worn out by the strain,
He lies spread on his back, with no help in sight.

By this surrender and intensive yearning
An answer comes; from God-flame ever burning.

II

In Adam's slumbering mind arose a dream
A warm consoling voice, a Father's call,
Saying "don't cry"; and then a brighter gleam
Of light unveils a scene which does enthrall.

It was an orient land. On darkest earth
A Sage sits smiling with firm and tender gaze
Saying "I'll help you, dear one, find rebirth",
His look is steady and his eyes ablaze.

It was as if some summer rain did fall
On this arid, parched and hard caked clay,
When Adam stirred from sleep he did recall
This dream, the lustrous dawn of Life's new day.

His prayer had been answered way down deep
Refreshed, his soul awakened from its sleep.

III

Adam heard within himself the Sage ask "Why?",
Speaking out of silence, so soft and clear,
"Ask yourself my child, the question 'Who Am I?'
You're not that body, insentient thing of fear

But Divine; a spark of sacred fire!
Quest within, search for that hidden flame,
Dive deep inside your Self, inquire!
Until you reach that One without a name."

Adam was free, his soul had found release
Joyful calm and ease enwrapped his heart
He now felt deeply One, at perfect peace
Forgetting all his past, to forge fresh start.

May the message in this dream, our Hope renew
To seek for Self within! Know That is True.

The Baptism

Trying to emerge
In the still white morning,
Glistening, clean.
Do not judge the things to come,
As yet, unseen.
God, father, mother,
Echoes of what we mean,
O do not name the silence
Words only come between.

Meet Me

Meet me by the lake of the sun
Where we will be light of heart
And no longer carrying burdens of the earth.

Meet me in the house of horus
Where we will be honoured guests
And no longer separated from our kin.

Meet me in the fields of immortality
Where we will carry our heads upright
And no longer stumbling on the path of peace.

Meet me in the heart of God
Where we will be fed on love
And cheeks no longer wet with tears.

Meet me in the treasury of light
Where we will know the mysteries
And be no longer seekers in the darkness.

Meet me in Jerusalem
Where we will be ourselves
And no longer suffering the lower masks.

Meet me through the eastern gate
Where a straight path will be prepared for us
And no longer needing to retrace our steps.

Meet me on the sacred shore
Where we will disembark in eternal sunshine
And no longer tossed on the waves of wayward passion.

Meet me in the promised land
Where all our company will be choice
And no longer scattered in the wilderness.

Meet me beyond the moon
Where the two lights will be as one
And no longer dimmed in a world of shadows.

Meet me in the sanctuary
Where we will be hidden to the eyes of the world
And no longer threatened by our enemies.

Meet me in the place of victory
Where we will be crowned with light
And no longer encircled by the powers of darkness.

Meet me in the fourth heaven
Where the new way begins
And no longer suffering the pains of birth.

The Players

Characters in an old remembered play,
Our friends and lovers slowly fade away:
They acted out their parts and so did we,
Unconscious of theatricality.

Experience has made us what we are:
Pain we avoid, reminded by the scar;
Though many trials by which we have evolved
Are now forgotten: memories dissolved.

The first unwise decision, broken vow,
The first rejection; all these things are now
Superfluous, as lines which when rehearsed
Were needed, but now unneeded, have dispersed.

So shall it be when we have gone the way
Of other roving players, to the clay:
When in new guise, we strut a different stage
In roles more elegant, sublime and sage.

Logos

There is but one song - the song of life,
There is but one voice - the voice of God,
We are the melody of God's Great Song,
Whose sound is Harmony, in Truth.

The Friend

Walk with me my gentle friend
For I am ears to hear you
And I am quiet, listening in
And I no longer fear you.
For you and I have travelled far,
And never known the reason
And now I see your bucksome pride
And now I know your season.
For you are fiercer than I guessed
And you are well endowered
And you are brighter at your best
And you are higher powered.
Walk with me my gentle friend
For I am ears to hear you
And I am quiet, listening in
And I want to be near you.

In This World

In this world
The beauty lies hidden
Beneath the oil, between the shells
On a million fossil-strewn, sand-grained beaches.

In this world
The truth lies waiting
Amongst the debris, in the broken eyes
On the pavements by a million abandoned tabernacles.

In this world
The love is still shining
Through the humility, through the despair
Of starving families in a million ramshackle shanty towns.

In this world
The heart of hope is still beating
Despite the trials, beyond the anger
Of the millions who are subjugated, who are degraded or abused.

In this world
The good is still there
Transcending the rest, life over death:
Feigning dormancy, a bright diamond in a terrible wasteland rough.

In this world
We must be good, my friend,
For our time is short, our options are few -
What we look for we will find, what we deserve we will receive.

Seven Fathoms Deep

One Voice and Seven Strings,
One Sun in Seven Rings,
One Breath through Seven Notes,
One Keep in Seven Moats.

One Eye through Seven Colours,
One King on Seven Horses,
One Father and Seven Mothers,
One Path with Seven Courses.

One Gold in Seven Metals,
One Water in Seven Vessels,
One Love with Seven Helpers,
One Peace and Seven Shelters.

One Lock with Seven Keys,
One Life in Seven Trees,
One Fire through Seven Lights,
One Day and Seven Nights.

One Truth through Seven Heavens,
One Alone and Seven Sevens,
One Beauty in Seven Veils,
One Freedom and Seven Jails.

One and Seven equal Eight
To help the Fire circulate.

Yours

Yours is my face, oh Sage
looking in
through this window
to this clear boundless space of no-thing I
evaporating dew.

Your contour, mountain and river,
is dissolved in planes of eternity.
Your Grace ever gazes steadfast
alive and bright
into this clear space of boundless no-thing I.

God is looking
deep into this cave.
He is sweeping out the dust.
God can reside here
formlessly.

How? Give over this sense of I
to I.
Eye to eye,
who is looking in?
And who is looking out?

The little toiling slave, putting
down a bundle of thoughts, welcomes air,
drawn up with dew.
How can I ever leave thee?
Where would I go?

The Soul's Odyssey

Beneath the helm of dark Orion's stare,
Upon the bosom of deep breathless Night,
The fiery comet wings its Mystic Way,
Its heralds wake, a stream of muted light
To the shores of distant Hesperus.

The far off flickering of a Cosmic Lamp,
Across the pregnant darkness of the Deep,
The sudden sparkle of a distant solar flare,
Holds a secret hard to keep...
The road to fair Elysium.

Within the swelling Womb of darkling Space,
A silent billow crests its frothy edge,
Then scatters in many a thousand sparks,
When dashed upon an unseen rocky ledge
Souls like specks of Sunlight.

Ah! What Breath stirred these Golden shoals,
Born to swim through winding Orphic Streams,
In subterranean caverns deep and hid from Light,
Till sorrow's scalding cut and Nature's means
Bursts its gentle Heart.

But then! To the Sunlight Young and Second-Born,
Astride the Phoenix in timeless Flight,
Carried breathless on its meteoric soar,
Singing freely through the Cleansing Light
Back to fair Elysium.

A Song! A song O Muse to sing,
Harmonic with its ringing edge a'quiver,
To join these Choristers in their dulcet rise,
To the dancing hem of Aurora's shimmer
That drapes the Gates of Heaven.

Swans

The throbbing of the wings
As they beat the air
Made heads turn upwards
And we stood to stare
At the long necks stretching
Straight to the fore
Wings moving slowly
Confident of reaching the shore

Born to the freedom of Earth and Sea
Bound by a love cloaked in majesty
They glide, dip and caress the air
With rhythm; grace and magical flair.
To meet, and thrust for the sky, they climb.
Unafraid to let their spirits shine
For an eternal love is what they share
That even death cannot impair.

Deceptive Reflection

I was real.
I knew I was real
because I could see myself in my mirror

There were signs of me all over the place;
My clothes in my wardrobe,
my writing on the page,
my car in the garage
which adjoined my house,
my bank account,
my birth certificate,

my national health number,
my numerous references,
my very good job,

my stable relationships
and my solid image.
You just could not miss me, I was so real.

Then it happened.

I broke my mirror,
and
the moths ate my clothes.
Arthritis seized my hands
as my car exploded
and my house caught fire.
I was bankrupt,
birth certificate gone,
national health number burnt,
references gone up in flames,
then the boss fired me.

My whole image was ablaze
and the self that I knew was reduced to ash.

I was dead.
I thought I was dead,
but I rose from the dust of the dying pyre.

Now I am.
I see what I am,
But it is not done with the aid of mirrors.

Simple Music

Green Holly, red berry,
Winter nips but I am merry,
Robin red, fields of white,
My heart is warm this frosty night.

Star bright, sky deep,
Comfort children while they sleep,
Clear drops, water's thunder,
Wash away the weight they're under.

Buttercup, sun-blaze,
Children laughing while they gaze,
Hawk's feather, needle Pine,
Help them drink the Mystic Wine.

Pigeons cooing, Peckers knocking,
Sounds of keys, doors unlocking,
Granite wall, mountain peak,
Reveal the Sacred Ones they seek.

Wind a'blowing, Poplar dancing,
Children of Life, Eye entrancing,
Kettle sing, crackle fire,
Simple music of the Lyre.

White horse, stone mound,
Signs of magic on the ground,
Pebble brook, river flow,
Dance of Life, melted snow.

Ice melt, eyes open,
Wisdom's here, no more groping,
Windows clean, petals wide,
Inner Flame with you abide.

Daisy Chain

Like a daisy,
Peaceful hearts radiate a thousand virtues
As masters' words warm a thousand hearts.

If One Breath inspires a thousand teachers
A calm eye centres a thousand breezes.

Oh then, a thousand mysteries of the All-Seeing!
May Truth, a thousand ways be told.

The Flame

I would say
That I love within you the sacred flame.
You just might say the same.
Then there is no interference or strife
With lines of life.

There is no captive
To possess.

Let it be in the Will of He
Who burns most bright in 'BE
STILL' within this heart.
Let the in-turning art
Of the Pilgrim
Be its offering to Him
Who is the receiver.
Burned there is, a most subtle savour
To the gods.

I would say
That in a sacrament I,
The pilgrim, lovingly am taken in the flame
That receives my name,
That is radiant and hidden and boundless
In the Being.

Patterns

Lying under a tree,
Is where I belong,
Watching, patterns
Form and go,
No need to use
These patterns,
Or do something with them,
No need to label
Each piece of grass
Blowing in the wind,
Or imagine that it dances,
Or has character,
No, that is not it,
The mind plays
A million tricks
And interpretations,
But what is there,
Cannot be told
In words.

Sage

The primeval Sage in silence sits
Emitting waves of God-Love to all those
Who rest surrendered at His sacred feet.
His mystic sight means He surely knows
How to destroy His devotees' mournful woes
That prevent their climb to a holy place.
His merciful aid abundantly flows
Ever to give pilgrim the power to trace
His Self ablaze in tranquil sea of grace.

Ode To The Frigate Bird

Oh! Sentinel of these southern seas; impervious to our plight
You soar aloft in majesty and hold us in your sight
Will you still be with us in the desperate days ahead
Do you offer hopes of landfall - or mourning for the dead.

For many weeks you've led the way, beating wings unblinking stare
Immortal spirit with us now e'er watchful o'er our bended brow
Your jet-black plumage graceful sight keeps eerie vigil through the
night
It seems to us that all is lost, as in this little boat we're tossed

This mighty ocean is your home, no walls or fences halt your roam
'Neath opalled wings to life we cling and wait to see what fate will
bring
With humble prayers thy warriors we, place our faith in destiny
God give us courage and armour me as we survive the savage sea.

A ship - A ship we voice the cry, Oh frigate bird don't let us die
Our pinnacle of contentment soared as eager hands hauled us on board
Now we rejoin the human race and sadness falls upon my face
Farewell my friend I'll ne'er forget thy black green feathers bold and set

On moorland hill now curlews fly, for many years have passed us by
Long remembered are those days, o'er curling wave where dolphin plays
As life's harsh conflicts bend my will, your inspiration guides me still.
And thoughts return to where you ply, the lonely sea - Pacific sky.

The Quest (From 'Songs Across The Desert')

To See with Single Eye the moving Drama,
To ride the Magic Horse of Passion,
To Penetrate the Net which binds us tight,
Through the Door of Liberation flashing!

One Moment

With your touch you fill me within.
With your smile you caress my heart.
With your love you radiate warmth.

> Somewhere softly
> A note is sung
> In memory, in mercy.

With a calmness you hold me still.
With a whisper you fold to my wish.
With a brightness we burn eternal.

Unseen Weaver

Here stands a giant loom of Time in duration,
It is born of Infinity from a whole consummation
With Life, which has ever been void of time.
The sun and moon as shuttle upward climb

By playing, weaving to and fro as night and day,
A splendid pageant of coloured display.
All is strung on warp and weft of cosmic unity,
The back of this vast embroidered tapestry

Is monochrome, derived from the formless One.
The face is multihued and radiant as Sun,
Its tones reflected from archetypal light
Unabsorbed, are an unequalled sight.

Only what's permitted by unseen hand
Appears as moving panorama, a horizontal band,
A magic painting of the whole wide world.
Brushed as vertical, each single thread is whirled

Without dimmest dint of dull duality
As Light, unique unto its Self. Sheer Reality!
Coated by golden fleece and white angelic wool,
It is dyed in deepest vat, destiny's darkened pool.

So does the holy cloth that's woven in Love
Quarrel with his weaver who rules from above?
Rather, wrapped in warmest cloak at rainbows end
Eternal pilgrim e'er adores his Mighty Friend.

Admonition

In the face of adversity,
Where is your Strength?
- Restore it.
As the cruel prey upon the weak,
Where is your Courage?
- Rearm it.
As the cynics tighten their grip,
Where is your Faith?
- Repair it.
In the sea of despair,
Where is your Hope?
- Refloat it.
As betrayal overcomes trust,
Where is your Loyalty?
- Befriend it.
As whims are indulged to excess,
Where is your Duty ?
- Follow it.
In the realm of pain and loss,
Where is your Compassion?
- Empower it.
As pride confounds the minds of men,
Where is your Humility?
- Embrace it.
As cries of need die unheard,
Where is your Kindness?
- Nurture it.
In the bound coffers of greed,
Where is your Generosity?
- Share it.
As sly deceivers see their chance,
Where is your Honesty?
- Unlock it.
As fools pick too soon the fruits of their endeavours,
Where is your Patience?
- Ripen it.

In the storms of turmoil,
Where is your Peace of Mind?
- Sustain it.
As corruption overcomes the pure,
Where is your Poise?
- Establish it.
As deserts encroach on the fertile plains of the heart,
Where is your Love?
- Outpour it.
In the deep well of confusion,
Where is your Wisdom?
- Understand it.
As brute falsehood vanquishes truth,
Where is your Judgement?
- Discern it.
As the shadows multiply across the face of the earth,
Where is your Light?
- Emblazon it.
In the uncertain future,
Where is your Past?
- Recollect it.
As stark choices have to be made,
Where is your Present?
- Decide it.
As the dream begins to fade,
Where is your Future?
- Desire it.
In the measuring of days,
Where is your Heart's Desire?
- Treasure it.

To Die

To die
Is to leave behind
The smell of fire,
A puff of wind,
The known for the unknown,
Leave the sun for darkness,
As woman follows woman
Into the womb of Mother Earth.
I a child unbelieving
Waiting for respect
Am earthed
On bended knees,
And cannot but remember
The hum of Mother Earth,
Peaceful power
That is, that moves;
I am quiet, calm,
Feeling what is,
Knowing something
Of what lies inside.
I am deep river
Inside the tree
Sinking roots into the ground
To grow.

The Voyage Of Life

When I started my journey, into the
Uncharted oceans of my fears
I knew not which way to steer
I was guided by hands that knew the
Waters of adversity.
Through the jagged rocks of guilt
And whirlpools of denial
Through the storms of avoidance
Powered by the will to succeed
The recognition and trust of my shipmates
Our sails filled with the acceptance
Of care, and together find a course
To the calmer waters of understanding
'A time to reflect'
Then! Look at the horizon
You wonder what is at the end of
The long and difficult voyage
What is the reward that will be there
When you reach your destination?
It is a 'jewel' that others knew was
Always there.
But you have to find yourself
Discovering that the greatest
Treasure of all is you.

Invitation

I am a pool, still and sweet
Centred in a garden of my own making
Take a stroll in my grounds
And you may find me
Gaze upon my surface
It may shimmer
And shine in the sun of your perception
Whilst in the dark, silent depths
Rests my heart
Feeding earth in peace and quiet
Dive in
And be cooled if you will
Emerge
And there you might see in a new light
My garden, quietly nourished
How fair the flowers would grow
Forget-me-nots and Pink Campions
In carpets of most subtle weave
Spreading their bright delights around
For those who may, to behold.

Sonnet On The Beach At Leigh

To detect my indwelling Sovereign everywhere
In mud and bird and ungainly human continent
Is praise of One in whom all hidden share.
So wide is this field to foot-fall made conscient.

Compassionate is the Sun's path to each inward light.
How may I judge this mystery of His currency
In the darkroom of two eyes that strive for sight?
Sea-birds nestling on sea-bed touch clemency.

Abandon prejudice! The quest of one heart, cosmic into other,
Is a lantern, bright hermit, aloft so gentle to behold
That in cloak of colours I grasp not, is in thee, my Brother-
Sister Self, Divine. In shadows of our hidden gold,

The Sovereign winging, oft mistaken, o'er shoreless ocean
Is surely pilgrim to a great Circle: an occult completion.

A Sestina "Te Deum"

Our hymn is sung to the Great and Wondrous One
Who dwells in splendour, a dazzling radiant light
That shines in every Heart and each manifest Sun
Of Self-effulgent beauty, blazing bright.
Thou art All, and Thy mighty will be done,
Oh make our actions worthy, in Thy holy sight.

Oh Lord, we pray to keep Thee ever in our sight,
Oh Thou whom we adore, our God the Holy One.
Your rays of Grace and Love are ever bright
In strength and power, as the awesome crimson Sun.
Oh keep us from all wavering, fix our Heart on light,
Thou art All, and Thy mighty will be done.

Thou art All, and Thy mighty will be done,
Not foolish will of ego, lest it darkens sight
And screens us from the bliss of Thee, oh Kingly One.
Thy blinding brilliance of eternity bright
Is stronger, deeper than the summer mid-day Sun.
Let us bathe in blissful balm of blessed light.

Oh lead us Lord, from nescient dark to conscious light!
Thou art All, and Thy mighty will be done
And ever mindful we are resting in Thy sight
For thou art Father, Mother, Teacher, Friend; oh Holy One
Your perennial fire is flaming clear and bright
Deep in the heart, a resplendent inward Sun.

He who within us hides and bides is also in the Sun,
Black clouds dispelled by beckoning beacon light.
On bended knee we glorify Thee, oh Primordial One
Who through Grace revealed demists this frosted sight.
Thou art All, and Thy mighty will be done
Polish the mirror of our Souls and make them ever bright.

Oh Jewel of Faith that ever sparkles diamond bright
And shines fiercely as our bosom friend, the Sun,
Thaw the frigid heart with warmth and light
Thou art All, and Thy mighty will be done.
Oh let our acts be worthy, in Thy holy sight,
A hymn to be sung to the Great and Wondrous One.

Praise to the Holy One, ever burning beryl bright,
May His wisdom light guide us as the Sun
And may His will be done, in His all loving sight.

The Holy Grail

Oh gather all we Seekers
Around the Holy Grail,
Oh hear its Sacred Teachings
With which we cannot fail.
Come! behold His Holy Radiance
Casting out all doubt,
Oh drink His blessed Waters,
To end this bitter drought.
Now Springtime of Creation
Fills all the Earth with Flowers,
The sky vibrates with Bird-Song...
The Heart with Secret Powers!

Embroidery

There is a seam of meaning
in all this,
crossing the smooth slope
of a slip stitch
piercing through the fabric's
crispness
starting something new.

A tapestry emerges
chained to a hum-drum thread
beige or grey or olive
imitating the real world of weaving.

In only the space of the needles eye
silkily sewn satin
binds the blankets edge
catching the roughness
of work worn hands.

Of course, it's a herring-bone,
complicated, twisted,
hard and
not always decorative either,
or french,

and there is a knot in the end
of the cotton,
but the hem was well made.

Swans At Night

The moonlight strikes the alder's crown
And lays its layers of silver on the lake.
In the shadows, purpled roses breathe
The evening air. White gleams of down
Amongst the willows' wicks, make
Augury for their entrance and the ease
Their stillness brings to anxious eyes.

The white fires grow, limn in their forms,
Until, like swelling images of dreams,
Two swans are burning on the lake;
Altar bright against the darkened thorns,
Calm in their strifeless self esteem.
Creatures watching from the shadows take
Heart at beauty in such a guise.

On Poetry

Created out of entropy,
In the poet's own mind's eye
And compressed;
To form the fabric
Of myths and stories
Of life and love and death.
A poem; or a parable
Plotting a parabola;
A caricature of truth.

But contained in these hyperbole
There is a gem - like purity,
That is not found in certainty;
Nor in probability;
Nor in the cold mathematics
Of real life.

Sunrise

In the dawning
chill world is the waiting
as Sage is rising
to dry the dew,
to warm this anxious world again with life.

The deer is bounding
through the glistening forest
soft eyed, alert
and as still as a tree.

Sage, thy coming is through the forest.
Thou art parting the leaves
with rays from thine eyes
golden.

Sun rises over the rim of the sea
and the world tenderly
is warmed.
If I am locked in my head
I starve and die.
If I open my heart
I may rejoice in the morning
and play with the deer.

The wise hunter hastens not.
The wise hunter waits
for the shy creature to appear.
Sometimes
joy spreads through the being,
as verily as did dark grief at night,
from ear to ear strengthening.

Such joy from the searching
glance of the Sage
may, striking my prismatic tear, soften the world,
shoot rainbows into this surrounding tissue
of fire and rain a gentle issue;
indescribable touch of colour there is

to lighten, to gambol in,
to whiten and brighten
this weathered field.
The deer is bounding
through the glistening forest
soft eyed, alert
and as still as a tree.

Then Sage, come.
Thine eyes are
nectar in this cave
of the heart.

Untitled

This is the voice of the un-sound
The controversial spirit within the ether
Of our inheritance
Teaching us to be human.
It is the quizzical within the rational
It is unheard, a breath exhumed
From the dead, who lay living
Under earth.

And movement stirs us,
Belonging to the steel and stone
Erect before us, unyielding.
We carry our bread and water.

Under a spell it speaks; we will
With an ignorance displayed
In grieving for flesh which sheds
And purges.
Unholy, our communion with cold stars
Blasphemy in wake
For gods whose names we swallow
For the want of power.

This is the voice breaking through the structure
Of a square world
Wishing to be round. Once
We were circles, reeling out
And meeting back again
For the beginning of our lesson.

Unharnessed this wind
Howling our distraction;
Words against the fracture
Voices for souls.

Initiate

When deepest words are wasted in the speaking,
And your aching Heart is silent as a frosted stone,
When your tired eyes no longer see the Wonder,
And on the stony Path you walk alone,
When the pain-filled Night seems to you eternal,
And still no Light seems there to be...
Then it's time to weigh the ancient anchor,
And cast your Barque upon the Inner Sea.

When no loving hand is there to soothe the brow,
And endless troubles oppress the Mind,
When words of comfort have flown the Winter,
Another deserving soul to find,
When all your Doors are surely bolted,
And your Wings lay languid in the Cage...
Give not your tongue to sorrow's bitter spite,
Nor on the cruel vent your rage.

When your Heart hath bled with scarlet sorrow,
And washed with life's blood the weary feet,
When all things seem but hollow shadows,
And the soul unwraps its winding sheet,
When deserted, lonely and despised,
And spoken of with slanderous lies...
Then send thou forth sweet Thoughts of Love,
And cleanse with Fire the blackened skies.

For Thou, another holds the Golden Keys,
And awaits your coming with outstretched arms,
For Thou, a greater Sun than Lights the Heavens,
Who with His Secret Peace all trouble calms,
For Thou, a precious Robe of Potent Love,
Most Sacred Fire of scarlet red,
For Thou, a Crown of jewelled Wisdom,
Glittering with Power upon thine head.

After Reading 'John Of Gaunt'

This 'golden seat' of wisdom's light
This haven of strength and measur'd ease
This ancient Oak well fed by roots
Sprung-deep from feet of clay
This trial of tears in mercy judged
This tillage of hearts that reap good Nature's cup
This forest that veils the timid deer
Amidst the baying chase
This buoyant raft that rides the swell
This twinkling-eye reflecting starry night
And this, the Ruby that surmounts the Emerald tide!
Whilst aspiring the setting of a higher crown
Its facets, beacon-bright, do warn against the storm
And summer-cut, in time, glow warm with benediction
In company with all the faery shades that captivate the eye
Oh, this bejewelled landscape!
This kingdom, this England of my being...
Constant and firm be thy heartland ever
And this, despite the ever-changing shore...

Ancient Tree

Ancient tree,
you comfort me.
I lean on your wisdom,
experience and strength.
You have known loss
and harsh weather.
You are a survivor.

Ancient tree,
you set me free.
You make no demands,
exert no pressures.
I come and go
and when I return
you are still there.

Ancient tree,
stand and be
a symbol of life,
growth and survival.
Beneath your branches
I feel encouraged.
You set an example.

Orpheus

Oh fairest of the gods thou art,
Arising from out the lake of sleep.
Shaking thy dewy locks that weave fair patterns
Upon thy rose-misted brow,
Leaping to thy feet
As sprightly as the meadow daffodils.
What splendour adorns thy beautiful face,
Like some radiant angel
Come forth from the sun.
How could the moth resist you?
As if some stately flame had wandered here,
Deep among this Earth of clay...
Where darkness like a heavy shroud
Veils the Inner Eye of humankind!

What duty calls thee here then,
Among these dreaming clouds called life?
And if thou would secret be,
Then answer me some simple enquiry:

Of what nature are those magic aromas
That waft about thy marble-like form,
Perfuming my drunken brain with ecstacy?
And what those warbling melodies
Which linger on in my perceptions,
Bringing holy visions of a Central Glory
More fiery pervading than the rest?
And yet, no end to this extension,
Like some potent all proceeding Light,
Penetrating each Mystic Veil like silken crystal
Which fringes the fountains
And chalices of Heaven.

Oh, God, let not my tinctured Tongue
Be stilled awhile,
Nor let Thy Holy Flame abandon me,

But Thy Fire send coursing
Through these lyric veins...
The Wine of Poesy!

Oh how Thy fruitful Essence blows aloft
Among the woven rays of Angels,
Whose fiery radiations
In a sudden rush of vibrant rapture
Have drawn me upward to a higher view...
Upon the glorious Wings of Inner Vision.
And yet, no static flight is this:
A blazing chariot hurled ever upward;
Ever ascending to higher kingdoms,
Like a fiery Thought
Borne on the wings of a spiritual lance,
Till at some point halting,
I cannot tell,
(The Mind being carried beyond all language)
We perched as it were in an Aureate Light,
Booming with the orders of invisible Rulers...
In the Light of God's Consciousness.
And everywhere vast multitudes of Holy Sparks,
Blazing within that Light of lights;
Each spark a choral heart of Love,
Filled with joyful, vibrant Life,
Singing for all Eternity...
When all at once,
The whole aflame with ecstacy
And song divine,
Went spinning in a blazing tumultuous whirlwind,
Bursting like some exultant sparkling fountain...
Across the diamond floor of God's temple...invisible.

Oh God, Thou art in all,
The beginning, the middle
And the end of all!

What shock of shocks
And sorrow's fruitful tears,
As like the lightning flash
Which dashing through the atmosphere
Finds its prison within the darksome Earth,
I fell far down into this waking dream
And felt again the weight of mortal clay,
That hangs like a twisting serpent
Around some heavenly stem...
Clinging tightly with its suffocating grip.

Oh Thou, Orpheus, a King of the Sun,
Thine answer have you given,
Yet in silence, never speaking...
Thy Living Lyre enough!

A Glass Mountain

Somewhere.
There is a shimmer,
a brilliance
almost unnatural
that,
unlike a distant mirage,
does not pale with proximity,
but shimmers still;
Crystalline.

A man craves perfection,
covets the ideal;
he strives,
strives,
never quite succeeds.

He comes in homage,
he comes in consolation,
and,
forgetting his futility,
he smiles
from the inside.

Sport

He is out today.
Every bird is singing his name
every tendril towards him yearns,
each drop of morning dew
reflects the ocean of his grandeur.
The curtain of blue has lifted
to reveal a glory of Sun resplendent.

Sometimes behind a gloomy cloud
He hides in mischief sulking.
But having glimpsed in undergrowth
the hem of his robe, I know
that he is somewhere about
and enjoying the play.

Look who just flew into the room
in food-moth form!
searching for a flame
in which to be consumed.

Sometimes you wrap
Yourself in a cloak of pain
to chisel away at my basalt rock
an image of thy Name

and other days you send
a Cup of nectar
for my honeybee soul to humbly sip.

Magnificat

Great Glory Given of Golden leaf
this day of autumn, rustles my living
Mystery, my awe and wonder
face

to the Original Face
no face of my own, this noble oak
who stands so magnificent,
adorned, space stretching
many branches, many limbs.

Mystery, my Tree, pours
suddenly forth his nectarous bounty
in a shower of magical golden light, as song of birds
Magnificat, boundless in my being, so blessed is He
held in these open arms outstretched
without end, from end to end
to drink.

Like one to scare the crows, I AM
planted in sharp tang of earth, this field
of worm and humus turned. This ground dark with rain
is drenched in readiness, pungent fresh
frost wind and woody flavours.
As Spring

through Song of Songs
is born again as bird to rise
through earth's sweet hymen
membrane to the Summer full of fruit and flower
my autumnal Tree in Majesty is crowned

with the Sun his leonine robe, thanksgiving
to the Fall; to Creation's seed so deep
into the Mother
dark tangerine from wide white sky.

Here, the celebrant standing
in full flame of kingship ripe for winter
dies deep into deepest well of Spring

acorn of his
Resurrection.

From stout stem of rivers flowing
woodiness, a knotty crust of worlds
harbouring teeming creeping populace of beings
to rest, devour, take root and swim
around the unfathomed pulse of his concentric core,
he opens, as an Anointed One upon the Cross, his limbs
rooted in dark secret soil to the fall of aureate rain.

I think that I upon this noble Tree
of Life, Magnificat,
am a leaf that is driven by the wind's spirit to change
Unchangingly.

Jack Frost

The pictures on my window pane
Are magical yet true.
Some look like crystal flowers
With shimmering drops of dew.

You can see a million snowflakes,
Each one designed with care,
And if you look real closely,
There is a snowqueen hiding there.

You will never see who paints them.
But for you they come no cost.
For that very special artist,
Is the one they call, Jack Frost.

Rain Of Joy

Rainbows reflect the miracle
of your smile.
Vibrant stars deliver the blinding light
that illuminates your tender devotion.
Adoration like mine is filed along
with morning: when grass loves dew
and moon hands over to sun.
Your scent is beckoned by the wind
which quickly travels to my side
and calls the day to close.
Now resting on the cushion of a cloud
our magic spell drives rain of joy to fall.

The Call

The day draws on, the light is dim,
Come Home my love, come Home,
Oh quit this painful sphere my Friend,
Come Home my love, come Home.
The Angels call with silvern sound,
The Treasure in their Hearts have found...
Come Home my love, come Home!

The youthful bloom on happy cheeks
Will not the years outwit,
Alone your Heart with Loving Dew
Will wash the stains from it.
So close your eyes and come to Me,
An Inner Light across the Sea,
Casting shadows far from thee...
Come Home my love, come Home!

So far beyond this darksome Earth,
Simplicity to find,
Away! above the flagging world...
The jailer of the Mind.
Now break the fetters of the soul,
As bells of Gold begin to toll,
Hear their peals of Freedom call...
Come Home my love, come Home!

The distant Light, a Guiding Star,
Shines bright Within your Cave,
Let not the stormy fruitless doubt
Drown it like a wave.
For Faith be eyes to what's not seen,
Unbending Will and Vision keen,
Which penetrates this painful dream...
Come Home my love, come Home!

To Gardens of Beauty and honey streams,
Come Home my love, come Home,
Unveiling Mysteries beyond all dreams,
Come Home my love, come Home,
Brothers and Sisters all as One,
Who trod the darksome Path long gone,
All sing this deep Inspiring song...
Come Home my love, come Home!

Mug Of Wonder

Brimful of my Self.
Sated but Free
Oh, Praise
be to
God
for
this Mystery

The Enraptured Nightingale

You have ravished my Heart
Oh my beautiful Beloved,
The honey of your speech
Hath charmed and moved me;
The smell of your skin
Is of mystical incense;
Your eyes leave me breathless,
Like soft radiant jewels
Glistening with deep enchantment;
Gleaming and glittering
Above the rosy peach-down
Of your lovely cheeks;
Your shimmering veil
Like a dragon-dream hath fallen,
Revealing the scarlet
Of your dew-drenched lips;
The wine of your breath
Hath disturbed my being
And your smile hath warmed me
As the rays of the sun,
And I am lost and bewildered
In the waves of your Love;
But my troubled Mind is soothed
By your soft careful hand,
As you lead me in Peace
To your still meadow Waters;
Fill the tomb of my Heart
With delectable aromas
And heal the dry desert
With your clear sparkling Waters...
And the black robe of my sorrow
Is torn in your Presence.

The Lake In The Hill Top

The sky, on a journey over the isle of Mull
Rained dense misty veils each day; save one
Which radiant bathing hill and deep glen full
Of rainbow's faery shimmer, revealed ray of Sun.

Then climbed I to a gleaming pointed peak
Of stone-chat heathery flank that soared to sky
And found in the summit high hid, a sapphire lake
Hues heaven's mirror shining; a deep dark eye.

I within that ancient stone-girt hill tip seeing
So bright, so lofty a welling Source secluded,
Plunged into its pocket to swim, as sky my being
Cold sweet watery shock; oh secret, denuded.

Dived I then down. Beneath surface, opening sight
Was blinded - underwater, the dark eye of earth
Brown peat unfathomed, heaven meet with night.
Where light is drowned, where may eye breathe?

Night's nescience so deep is but chalice to raise
Hill high to the sky of sunshine deep and blue.
Like a young child who at Genesis insouciant plays,
Gazes face into radiant Face reflecting true.

Creation entering the deep and watery womb
Is seed of fire that is swimming within the tomb.

Life

Life, hold me by your strings
Dangle me from maypoles
Let the dancers swing me
Through the spring
Damp me, meadow-moist
In dawns
Climb me slow
To secret rocks
There shine me sacred
With the stones
Drink me in puddles
Roll me in rivers
Flow me lonely to the
One-legged heron
There, leave me.

Love me, love me,
With fellows and fishermen
With friends who
Lick, kiss, tickle,
And really <u>do</u> sing in the rain.

Life, hold me by your strings
And swing me high
And swing me low
And life, my faithful,
When you let me go
Please
Would you do it

Ever

Ever

So gently.

The Bamboo Flute

Pools of blue
dark depths of richness
Lifting, lilting
separating in a chorus of green
Splitting the air with melody
surfaced from the soul
Earth, air, fire and water
blended into nature's harmony of truth
Droplets circling, merging, flowing
held forever in eternity
Yet ever changing form

Energies dancing, sparkling fireflies
dripped as nectar from the liquid sun
whirling green and gold with life forces
spiralling upward from the earth
Heralds of love and beauty
there to greet the seeing eye of innocence
All echoing, sounding the one note of being
the music of creation
Plucked from the strings of the heart.

Desert Hills

In desert hills
I saw a tree of perfect symmetry
regal and alone
its fiery crown ablaze but uncharred
forcing hot vapours to surge heavenward
in a tumult of sacred energy.

Presence Meets Presence

The Lord of my heart
Is not to be reached by my
Hunting Him through Space,

Nor is He to be
Trapped by my waiting through Time
For Him to appear.

Even if I change
From one state to another
He will stay hidden.

The One I seek is
Spirit, present within change,
Always, everywhere.

This Presence is not
Dependent on anything
I think, say or do.

The only wisdom
That will help me is to be
Fully what I am.

When I, myself, am
Fully present here and now
He reveals Himself.

Presence meets Presence,
Person meets Person - within
And despite all else.

Virgo Rising To Virgo Sun

Sometimes to you I fly a little too close
to the Sun.
My wings melt.
Fall gravity into the drowning sea.

Then I must remember
from what Source, from Whom
irradiates that light; to which
we both seek to return.

Fly inwards to thine own
Sun rising
Guru's Grace
heart bathing.

See, it is a vestal lamp we bear
in whose stem is stillness,
whose tall flame wavers not:
Who am I?

Carry the lamp
into the cavern.
The silvery stem of the fire
is the water of life infinite.

Carry the lamp
in the oracle of the Earth
The body is a core most
ever melting.

Carry the lamp
towards the Sun.
The Sun is lighting it.
The flame has gone white into the day.

Who art thou?
who am I.
Flame drinks the wick of its
Self, steadily.

Vestal lamp held in virgin cave.
Point of stillness in Heart dissolving.
Sage of peace maintaining
Ears of wheat arising

green spears of grain golden ripening
from dark Earth.
Witness the rising
most slow, of the Spirit.

Witness tears that rain,
joy that shines and warms,
thunder and fog igniting despair,
the chills of winter which gestate the seed

impartially, with compassion.
Lord, I am a beggar in this field
standing ragged,
my arms outstretched.

The Dance Of Life

Reflection. Shadows.
Behind an invisible mirror.
Holding the veil masks.
Swayed to the sound,
The billows of the sea.

Moving images, Fantasy Fiction.
Reeling above carpet, pink feathers.
The spectrum colours.
Illuminated the stage.
The Four seasons.

The Autumn dance.
Golden leaves, Crinkling.
Naked trees. Cold breeze. Vibration.
They lost their dwelling,
Tracing footsteps on the homeland.

On the top. The tree of existence. A clock ticking.
On the other side the boundless fence,
The Spring was approaching.
All ready to dance,
Aspire to form a nest at once.

A glow of lightning.
Piercing through swinging clouds.
A logo of a footmark
Sealed by a sunbeam.
The word dance, engraved on the glass.

Beyond the passageway.
The licence was honoured.
The keynote, revealed,
Ready to perform, praise,
The dance of life.

From "He Feedeth Among The Lilies"*
Part IV

Lover:
"How fair, how beautiful you are, my darksome darling dear,
Your eyes that smile behind your veil are doves,
Your raven locks are flocks of goats in sheer
Descent from snow-capped Gilend in droves.

Your teeth are like a herd of sheep short shorn,
Come up from washing in pure Jordan's streams,
Each with twin lambs, is blessed, not one unborn,
Your lips a ruddy scarlet thread that gleams,

Cheery cheeks are peachy pairs of pomegranate
Demure within a veil of windswept fields,
Your neck is like King David's tower of granite
Upon which hang a thousand warrior's shields.

Your twin breasts, as pair of soft young roes
Fondly feed among the lovely lilies white
Until dawn breaks with tender colours of the rose
And darkest shadows flee before the light.

I'll rise and reach her magic mountains of myrrh
And her holy hills of fragrant frankincense
There is no flaw in her, so fine, so fair,
From Lebanon, my bride of higher mind and sense!
From Lion's lairs and Leopard's craggy haunt
You ride to ravish heart, my sister, bride,
With one quick flick of your glancing eye, you flaunt
The jewel which chastens awes my stubborn pride.

Your lips sip sweetness as the honey comb,
Milk and honey lie latent 'neath your tongue,
The fragrance of your royal robe is fresh as foam,
A rose garden sealed is my bride so young.

Enclosed by crystal spring and sparkling fountain,
Cinnamon scent of orchard fruit and Orient spice
Stream down the slopes of the sacred mountain,
With aloes, henna, nard and saffron rice."

Beloved:
"Awake, north winds, and gently harden
My plants, blow winds softly when it suits,
Let my dear Lover enter my secret Garden
To taste so quiet and still, my favoured fruits."

*A free version of the Song of Solomon

Joy

In watching the caged bird
Suddenly delighting
In the unexpected ecstasy
Of breasting the morning air
On this raw winter's day.

Russian Doll Theory

If there is placed within Nature
A Beauty of subtle rhythm
There is placed within Beauty
A Truth of simple greatness.

If there is placed within Truth
A Freedom aware of duty
There is placed within Freedom
A Heart Alive to itself.

Dana

Daughter of eternal Good and mother of its light
Bring forth from out of Self's own centre
The morning's child and darling of the sun.
My throat is all afire in search of you
And my tongue stutters out your holy name.
Smile now on your children lost in the night
Reach out your hand to them in their darkness,
Disperse with May-sweet breath their darksome thoughts
As you disperse the meadow-mists at morning time.
Lead us, yea lead us all to your cauldron of hope
That all our being may flow in one magnetic stream.
Then will we take our boats to the billowing sea
And as the milky way shines its peaceful path
We will cross the waters of the night-time sky
To disembark on new-day golden sands.

And to lead us on our half-known way
Flood once more the earth with your blue-eyed sons
That through their song we may remember thee.
Let not unbelieving scorn approach you,
Nor lift your ancient veil to baneful doubt,
But dispense your fire to the worthy ones
So we may hear again those souls aflame
Singing your praise in magic melody
Giving new life to your best-loved arts
Healing the broken heart of everyman
Scattering the fruit of your hazel tree
Soaring high on the wings of prophecy
Ever upwards, likewise ever inwards.

A Journey On An Island

I was walking beside 'forget me nots', red poppies,
Stood like the Queen's guards,
Wearing black, red uniforms.
Ready to join the armed force,
To salute the king of the universe.

A horn cry. Victory, defeat,
The imitation sound of trumpets,
Shattered by a shot gun blast.
A flock of screaming birds crossed over my head.
It was a matter of life, death.

A blazing smell filled the air.
Watching the burning bush,
I could hear the echoing sound of the lions,
Roaring at their dead victims,
Like terrifying avalanche of tumbling stones.

I crossed the lake by my boat,
The one in the shape of my lip.
Yearning to sail to the world of desire, grace,
To the rough world of my thoughts,
Where capital letters stand like peacock feathers.

Walking alongside soft sand, just like warm blanket,
Clamber to the top of a hill, shaped like a curved knife.
Beside, pink mushrooms, beyond endless carpet, Autumn leaves.
I could hear the chanting sound, church bells.
The sound of relief, piano tune of halleluia.

I sat down, leaned against a tree.
Inspired, wished I could play the tune of love on my veins.
Strive to reach up to that cloud, in a shape of a star,
To witness, splendid sight.
Glorious red balloon drowning into the sea.

Pilgrimage To Chartres

I

The glory of God's gospel gleams with light
Pilgrim sees growing from green of his ground
A tall temple of stone hewn high on her mound.
Her sculptural craft astounds his purblind sight
He bows down in surrender with all of his might.
He's awed by the magical joy of her sound
Angels chanting psalms, windows burning bright,
A new Jerusalem, the City of God, re-found!

Each niche tells a legend set in tinted glass
In radiant rainbow hue that sparkles as dew
For the mind that reads inward, a message so True.
Pilgrim feels healed by visions that pass,
His soul stands pure, no beam blurs his eye,
His heart uplifted to dear Christ in his sky.

II

Her spires aspire as arrows aimed at God.
Prayers assault her vaults, and heaven's reached,
The soul's inflamed to fire in earthly clod
By saintly sages who from oaken pulpit preached.
A medieval miracle, marvel to behold!
Be amazed! a maze on her lime stone floor,
Many parables her crystal panes unfold,
And stand in awe before her portal door.

To calmly comprehend this *art* in Chartres
So some cryptic chrism be unveiled,
Start to *chart* her craft with all thy heart,
In wise Christian mystery much is revealed.
Her stained glazed prisms gleam as gems
And pipe celestial hymns from which Truth stems.

III

Ah Chartres, *mystere merveille,* enigmatic book
Of God's creation; you're an emblematic sign.
Architectonic your binding, majestically Divine,
Your pages etched, alchemic glass; so look
For graven keys in carved and buttressed rock.
He points the path of husbanding the vine,
The way the holy Saints and Martyrs took,
A miracle, turning wan water into wine.

On flags of limestone lies a cryptic maze
Soul's riddle, puzzle whereby she's caught.
Once dancing here, an unknown Templar taught
His masons measured pace to freedom's ways.
In Chartres' arches clues are gladly given
For light! and tunes for sacred songs to heaven.

IV

Dig down deeply, dive in Self and find
A Chartres Cathedral of the inner heart,
The real temple bides behind the mind.
Stab the stony slabs of sleep, and start
To plunge within thy cryptic well, hold breath,
To thy sanctum sanctorum in right transept.
Sight seeing alone shall lead to death,
Seek Christ within, be templared and adept.

Notre Dame de Chartres mirrors the One inside,
From Self is thrown this temple on masonry wall,
The 'Light of the World' behind his door does hide,
So step beyond the shades, uncover all!
The Kingdom of Heaven shines within, not out,
Real Chartres waits in thy Heart; so turn about.

Haiku

'so profound is love,
that the heart challenges words
to convey its truth'

Identifying

The mickle and muckle cauldron pools
Are lying in their beds
The harvest moon and dawning sun
Raise each in turn their heads
And sweet primrose with morning's dew
Sit meekly side by side
As impenetrable forests
Of explorable pines
Are standing, still and high
The splashing lynn, the silent waves
Run then, hand in hand
The star filled eye and gentle rills
Leap both, to catch the tide
And skylarks sing and buzzards wing
Their ways in flight so high
With delicate adjustments made.
My mind likewise would soar,
Rising ever upwards, onwards ever
Free as the birds above.

Your Name Explained

In the wood where names are lost
hiding in holes, like the first mammals,
you wander, searching for a word,
some holy explanation. The name
is in the search.

Mystic Marriage

When Self has dipped her downy wings in Love
She begins with breathless joy the homeward flight
From here unto the sunny realms above
Where princess-pure she's crowned with gentle light
And all her trembling Being doth glow
Within the shining love-thoughts of her Lord
Which spangling down from Him to her doth flow.
Estranged till now, she is to Him restored;
Apart no more, she is by Him made Whole.
Her raptured heart doth melt in His embrace
(Blessed mystic marriage of Mind and Soul)
Truth now joined with Beauty, Virtue one with Grace
And all the precious tears she's shed throughout her life
Are blest, for they've made her now His eternal wife.

An Excerpt From 'To Future Nightingales'

May the words of thy tongue be beautiful and true,
Like heavenly fire-birds from Golden Star Island,
Who armed with golden quills of fire
And girded with the blazing breastplates of the Sun,
Come swiftly sailing on bejewelled Wings of Power
Through purple clouds of precious incense shining!
Sent forth by the fragrant Breath of the Holy One,
Across vast unconscious gulf of dreamy Neptune,
Whose moody Waters capture less vital thoughts
And drown them in the deep brooding flood of Sleep.

A glorious, vital and Immortal flock,
Blazing with splendour; electric and keen;
Who penetrate with unaffected Joy the heavy fog,
That hangs like some leaden, weary forgetfulness
Around these Plutonian entrance doors of earthly wit.

Oh, how should I say that these Victorious Birds
Have the Power to Remember and slay regret:
With living Songs, wherewith to mount the Winged-Steed
And o'erleap with fiery Enthusiasm
The barricades of the Mysterious Moon;
With Simple Truths, dressed in fascinating Veils,
Calling forth the mighty hosts of shining Thoughts
And all the Spirits of Imagination
From unsuspected Wells of Vital Consciousness;
And with Beauty, cleansing the grimy windows of the Mind
With pure liquid gem-drops of sparkling Life,
That now all things are bathed in Holy Flames...

As if some black-velvet Cave were opened wide
And in a sudden flash the Sacred Veil be torn!
And Lo! a breathless Treasure of Gold and Silver,
Of beautiful Gems beaming with Wonder,
In gleaming flames of red, green and blue,
Gush forth in waves of undreamt-of Riches!
And the Mind doth melt in Deep Enchantment...
In sacred Flames of overwhelming Love;
Unfolding the secret flowers of mystic
...REMEMBRANCE!

Everytime

Everytime
I lose in love,
I fall apart,

Into
A thousand
Love poems.

Mystic Fire

"To the Great One, the Strong in his Force, the Waker in the Dawn, to Fire as to one who has vision, let your hymn arise."

Hymn to Agni, Rig-Veda. Mandala I, Sukta 127, Vs.10. *

Our hymn we sing to Him in mystic fire
Blazing fierce with golden scarlet flame,
Flickering tongues to heavenly heights, aspire
To glorify the formless sacred Name.
All hearts turn to mystic fire, and inspire
Our souls like glowing coals, the same.

Our souls like glowing coals, the same,
Are lightning leaps of orange orient fire.
The thundrous clap helps humbled hearts inspire
To surrender ego dark in florid flame
And purify, bathing in lustrous lakes of Name:
To consummation does our quickened soul aspire.

To consummation does our quickened soul aspire
To find the One of Fame, always the Same,
And worship; surrender to His hallowed Name
And sacrifice prim pride in white-hot fire.
Transform, burning dross by inner flame.
Inward turning, does our pilgrim soul inspire.

Inward turning, does our pilgrim soul inspire
To God-Heart, making arrow-soul aspire
And wax warm worshipping with candle flame
To reach that Oneness evermore the same.
All change is wrought about by mystic fire
Renouncing arrogance for formless holy Name.

Renouncing arrogance for formless holy Name,
By hymns to mystic fire, our souls aspire.
The spark within fans fierce as fearless fire
To God; the blazing brand abounds to inspire,
And brightly burns to learn his Oneness is the same,
As naked fire immolates in flickering flame.

As naked fire immolates in flickering flame
We bow and chant soft praises to thy holy Name
'Till crimson dawn awakes and we become the Same.
So pilgrims, let hymns of mystic fire inspire,
To God, may our joyous souls aspire.
Be chastened in thy crucible of mystic fire!

Inspire my soul; Lord God aspire;
Become One, be same as formless Name
In sacred flame of holy mystic fire.

*Trans. Aurobindo.

Seeds Of The Virgin Moon

Across my aweful gaze you draw
your silver mantle
Clasping me deep within
your mysterious embrace
Drowning me deep within
your uncharted world

You challenge me to tread
the narrow paths
Winding through the labyrinth
of your heart
Your cool light stirs within me
ancient memory

A bond of familiarity locks us close
in swaying harmony
We dance the dance of time
long since forgotten
Stepping to untold rhythms
rising from our depths

Lost in endless motion
we touch each others knowing
Tears of joyous realisation
falling like silver rain
Down to kiss the dark brown
nourishment of earth

From where they meet and fuse
in moonlit glow
Spring seed of Being
magically manifest

Lying rapt in quivering anticipation
of Nature's stirring
They hold within each one
the pattern and promise
Of future golden days.

The Harvest

Sage, thou comest
with thy deft Scythe
to harvest golden stalks
of corn ripe standing
and reap essence

like a ray of Sun which comes
through the morning of thine eyes
receives this I awakening
to dry the dew.

*"For they give each
unto the other."*

Midwinter

Here on the hinge of the year
an April day,
a velvet wind, a southern sun
mocking midwinter,
tempting sticky-buds to glisten and unfurl,
the mute blackbird to sing its summer song
on a brief December day.

Here on the hinge of the year
a false hope,
but the trees, the silent bird resist
the mirage summer.
Grim winter has yet to nose out each hidden flower,
pick at each shoot with crystal stinging fingers
before April can flaunt its treasures.

Here on the hinge of the year
a glimpse of Spring,
a promise that the phoenix will rise
from the ruin of Autumn
to jewel each naked tree with gems of blossom,
transmute lead skies into the golden sun,
freeing through Winter's prism the firebird colours.

Pilgrims To The Sun

When Love has burned to ash all selfishness
And the sombre shroud of death is torn,
When inner peace has calmed all violence
And standing free we greet the dawn.
When broken are the bonds of sensuousness
And the jailer gives up his stolen key,
When the child within slays arrogance
And companionship turns I to We.
When goodness breathes its golden fruitfulness
And stirs the matter of our sleeping minds,
When trembling self steps into radiance
And entry unto heaven finds.
Then all our pilgrim tears and all our pilgrim sighs
Will be forgot, as Pilgrims to the Sun we rise.

A Land

You see love, there is a land
where love need not be spoken,
where Awareness only is,
and I ask thy hand
for my own to hold
in the ascent of this step
into shining clear space
mountain-girt
of Grace.

Here my love need not be in the telling.
Here my idea of thee is enrolled.
Here the Sage Being is felling
all that glitters and is not gold.

I Winter Speak

I frozen be
and chilling hoarfrost breathe
on forms suspended now
within my cold embrace

I time of pewter stillness
silver moon
and sprinkled stars
on deep-pile velvet blackness

With naked tree shapes
gaunt yet proud
soul-nature theirs, bare-offered now
as gift for those with eyes to see

So-near skies, grey veiled
enclosing earth
in deep-thought stillness
lifeblood...slow...flowing...go

Iced glace ribbon streams
crisp winding now
life, heavy-sleeping, hidden there
beneath cold stone

I winter-wash rich hues of Autumn
to blue misty muted tones
with earthself sepia-hard
bleak surface of apparent void

Yet seed-sown heart
lies warm within
and lifespark glow
stirs being into becoming forms

Herein all-time mystery lies
life-death-turning wheel
gives birth to children of the Light
from silent rest-time.

The Spirit Of Winter

I stare out through the frosted window
To observe a glorious scene of immaculate beauty
Acres of land, covered by a sea of unbroken snow
Nature at its most natural, transcendent infallibility

A flutter of snowflakes drop gently to the frozen ground
Covering the spectral limbs of the naked trees
The stark landscape is seductive, a season completely unbound
A hyperborean world, silent but for a stimulating breeze

I leave the man-made warmth of the cabin
To embrace the bleak paradise, ignorant of inclement weather
A solitary figure, striding over seasonal glaciation
Losing oneself totally, in the resplendent Spirit of Winter.

All Subsists In All

Happy pilgrim walked through the wintry night
Toward the altar of the rising sun
While Soma glanced across the sky to Venus
Transmuting snow to jewels beneath his feet.
And as day dawned amid the gentle hills
He breathed the electric breath of God
Blending his little spiritual light
With the blazing beacon of our Lord
Until his thoughts as pure as pristine snow
Reflected jewelled light within his mind.
And lo, how burning night and burning day
Rose like pillars of fire from the burning earth
To lift the blessed throne of perfect peace
Unto the shining palace of the sun
Where Remembrance bears the self away
On flashing oceans of enchantment
To shores divine where wisdom dwells with love
And priests of light compose their flaming prayers
Amid the sound of angel alleluyas
That echo soft as whispers of the Soul
When exiled mind is chained to lower earth.

Child

Horizons breath on soft pale skin
Innocence enveloping moon-like grin
Dreamscape knowledge on unfettered brow
Audacious gestures ingenious somehow.

Incandescence

There is fire in sapphire stone and fire in heart,
In hearth's glowing grate, in passion's flower
And night watchman's light house tower.
Flame is in sacrifice, in goldsmith's art,
In forked lightening's storm of thundering power,
In pinkly blushing dawn's awakening start,
In white hot lava within its molten part,
In scarlet sunset's tumbling twilight hour.

Fire scatters galaxies as seeds of grain,
Constellations are diamonds in His heavenly crown,
The comets dancing, as stars are gazing down,
The milky way's a lustral bridal train,
Waltzing whirling walking on an astral plain,
Suns light up streets in this celestial town.

There is fierce fire in germ of golden grain,
In soul of kindly King who sports a crown,
In neck of swan that's sliding river down,
In monstrous belch of engine hauling train,
In glowing windows of everybody's town,
In fire-flies flickering by dark in verdant plain,
In stormy clouds proudly pregnant 'fore the rain,
In angry rage of a self-righteous frown.

Fire lies in stems of roses ruddy at heart,
In bees who sip at pollen's virgin flower,
In war torn ravage of a blazing tower,
In autumn leaves tinted by nature's art,
In magic moments of the witching hour,
In these wonders fire wields a potent part.

The fire flares golden in fine flaxen flower,
As divine spark shines in every heart,
The flame of genius fans the painter's art,
Fire hides in God who holds such power,

In pent up horses before the races start,
In swift descent of angels in a blessed hour,
In volcanic burst viewed from lofty tower,
In each life-spirit fire plays His part.

He acts when an evil house burns down,
He's wild in wrath and wastes a wicked town,
He burns useless stubble from the harvest plain,
He bakes the bread that's worked from winnowed grain,
He inspires the gracious Sage his votaries to train,
In Kingdom of Creation, Sacred Fire is Crown.

Apollo's Garden

I enter the ethereal forest of dreams
An enchanted garden of peace and tranquillity
A realm of tender flowers and living streams
Home to Elves of age-old chivalry
And sylphen fairies of unrivalled beauty
I wander through this world of infatuation
My mind lost amidst echoes of Romantic poetry
I could live forever in this mystical imagination
Safe, away from the claws of man's devastation.

I sit amongst rows of violets; purple and white
Resting in this bountiful woodland haven
Beneath the ever-burning globe of filtered light
I dwell on the many glories of this realm; Arcadian
And realize that I do not want to leave Apollo's Garden
I need to stay eternally within his natural domain
In comparison to man-made hell, this is heaven
So, I close the portal to humanity's plane
And stride into the forest of dreams, to begin my life again.

The Inner Voice

From the depths of being comes the cry
Long and loud and never ceasing
Its echo rebounds from the walls of the heart
With empty longing
The voice is known, it's one that has been
Sometime heard before
It calls with memories of the past,
Stirrings of the present and future hope
It cries "I am Alpha and Omega, the beginning
And the end
The circle of my completeness and you the beloved
Companion on my journey
Together we will travel the open road
That leads to knowing and to destiny
Learning from each other,
Creating together that which is to be
And now, we smile upon our child,
The progeny of our listening"

A Poem To The Future

When our seasons part
Like fallen lovers
When our rivers dry out
To the deserts

I'll build a boat of clouds
With winged oars
And sail away
To fish for starlit ambers...

Sacred Truth

In your smile
I am born again,

In your eyes
All hopes and dreams return,

In your love
There is infinite peace,

Such magic
Comes but once,

Such truth
Is surely sacred.

Memories Of May

Like the blackbird's shining beak at the dawn of day
A honeyed beam shone forth from the eastern gate of night
To kiss the earth who, wrapped in snow, yet dreamed of May
When she, all decked with emerald grass and blossoms bright
Doth dance the dance of heaven and doth fill the air
With perfumed memories of aeons long ago
When sun and she their bliss in paradise did share
And all her rushing streams with jewelled life did flow
Through meadows of gentleness, through leas of light and love,
Through secret glades of sanctity and solitude,
Through hills of inspiration that towered above
Her hallowed plains of inner peace and certitude.
So if thy frostbound mind doth dream of long-lost May
Then go within and seek the inner source of Day.

Myrobalan Of The Magi

OH LOVER, look clearly to the palm of my hand
See thy chrystalline nectarine fruit;
I hear Orphic strains hymned by thy flute.
Let me go crazy with joyous ecstacy! and
Get drunk on spirit-scalding fire, fanned
By September's blissful breeze. Deep at root
Of thine etheric heart is an emerald shoot
Of the primal Sage who taught by silence in an ancient land.

There's a myth of emblic mystic myrobalan.
It's sacred as the palm, the rose, the mandrake
Whose fragrances graced the Galilean lake
Flaked by Solomon's lilies, of which the lamb
Of God spake; for his dear disciple's sake.
"Be still, and know I am God, That I Am."

White-gold Sun

Past green-gold fields on wheels of speed,
all through the summer afternoon
we take the long straight roads new-made
beneath a golden sun.

Beyond the fields, trees golden green,
moved to sing by a sighing breeze,
as incense to the white-gold sun
exhale a haze of heat.

And yews with hearts of darkest green
edged with blue by far-off magic
wait for ev'ning's shadows long
beneath the silver sun.

The God I Worship

The God I worship, lives outside,
In every river, every stream,
In every fresh green meadow,
In golden fields of grain,
In every living rock and stone,
In every hill, and mountain high,
In every bush, in every tree,
In every flower and blade of grass,
In every single bird that sings,
In every creeping crawling thing,
In every creature of the earth,
And in every fish that swims.
Deep within the ocean depths,
And high amongst the clouds.
Not in some damp and musty church,
But in the hearts and minds of men.

Aurora

The morning glow of golden hue is born
The cocks do crow in carillon call
The dark's dispersed by streaks of crimson dawn

Hear choirs of birds carolling hymns for all
To lift awareness up as opening eyes
Greet new day. Soul growing tall

And wide awake, attention inward flies
To seek Self in Heart this blessed morn,
The Self a blazing light that never dies.

Wavespeak

My ever changing form
kneels to the moon
At the mercy of her
cool ivory rhythms

She draws me to her
releasing rocks from my tenuous grasp
Then, with her outbreathing
Spits me out
on waiting land-forms

By night - unseen
Moonflowers drip like honey
to my heaving depths
My task - to nurture them
Then, to spew them forth
Love gifts, nestled in
crisp lace silver foam

For those with eyes to see
I leave them
Strewn on a waiting seashore
until an open heart receives them
Treasures of time past
and seeds of new beginnings.

Magic In The Moors

I love the days when the moon is round
and the stars are here for the night;
when the sea is blue from the breath of a prayer
and the sky burnt dawn breeds delight.

I love the dream when the sun is soft
and the frost creams the light with joy;
when the crackle of stars from fresh frozen grass
makes the curious earth seem like sky.

I love the song of a car-less land
where the air is pure with brave life;
when the moorland boasts of a landscaped bliss
and the power of hope meets belief.

I love the touch of a winter's sigh
as the snow filled clouds hide the sun;
when the sure footed sheep climb the triumphal tors
and all nameless fears are overcome.

I love the smell of the ice gripped soil
on the banks of a fast flowing stream;
when the wild water swirls round the granite grave rocks
speed-full from a recent storm.

I love the peace of this English scene
in the echo that wakes my soul.
Not a hint of discord is allowed to brood.
Not a wayward dread to console.

The River Of Honey*

Beneath the gaze of the pitying stars
A lonely caravan winds its mystic way
Towards the golden East - Oasis bound
To fill their empty water flasks with Life.

And on the way, amid the stinging wind
A child arrives, an hour before the Dawn.

Rejoice! And Praise be to the Treasury!
Tomorrow we will deck our tents with turquoise
And sprinkle honey and water on new sown corn.
We will feed on honey cakes and honey bread
And feast with kin on heaven's ripened date.
We will smear the new born's lips with honey
And hide virgin honey beneath his tongue,
Rub all his limbs with ointment from the Sun
And keep away the chilling winds of heartache
With salves of honey and wine and butter bright.

* '...and the angel brought me to the river of
    honey...' (Apocryphal New Testament)

Heaven Is In Your Heart

Beyond my house there lies a dale
Which leads onto the moors
And, yearning for its pensive trail,
Today I put aside my chores.
As I climbed towards the peak
I beheld a winter scene
The sort that tourists often seek,
Refreshing, crisp and clean.
Sunbeams danced upon the frost
Neath a mantle blue and clear,
Like a remnant of a Paradise lost
With an air of Christmas cheer.
Rejoicing in each sight and sound
I became with them a part
But realised that the Heaven I'd found
Was a feeling deep within my heart.
And this world that I'd thought separate
From some Heaven far away
Was no longer lost and desperate
But God's reflection on display.
Then I prayed with all my might
That this kingdom found within
Would shine forth as a beam of light
In a world perceived by most as dim.
Standing on the moors this day
Truth was revealed to me
And it took my very breath away
With its bold simplicity:
Heaven is just a state of mind
As Hell is, if we choose,
And each is there for all to find
With all to gain or lose...

On Discovering The Beloved

The Soul is tasting
salt,
this salt, being crushed and pressed
in the mayhem as the waves one, two, high *Hokusai*
crash over the bed of this soul
that is tasting the Salt

like a child does, venturing into ocean to dive
before being born.
The Soul is tasting salt.
It is just; she just is swimming.

I heard in my dream a boy child cello.
The prodigy raised over the strings his bow
to play Bach
but there fluttered out like a bird
so pianissimo
Elgar Second movement questing.
And the wave came
high like a mountain range, and creaming,
and over my body sitting here, it broke,
crushing I, thrashing water, snapping timbers
breaking my house, drowning breath

and yet under that titanic weight
of power and chaos boiling white, and destruction,
I live. I witness.
And two times the boy prodigy raised his bow to the strings
and two times the opening bars of Elgar fluttered out
and two times the high wave came,
broke over me, crushing me
before I woke.

This Soul, this soul is tasting the salt
that pours from the eyes it seems,
and some brief that this Soul has before birth
is for surrendering to the pounding
of that breaking wave.

In strange timeless delight my Soul doth taste
sharp, the sea
she enters,
as a child does, swimming.

In the agony of time passing
over the heart, broken, speech prohibited
for the fragment of love,
wooden, silent, straining, snapping, there is nothing
but the searing pain
of seeing thee and not reaching.
Strange detachment now enters. Thou art
but one fragment of this whole love
that cannot be spoken, this grief which devastates,
child beside me who is crying out,
can my child in the water wild still see me?
Am I still here?

In strange timeless delight my Soul doth
acknowledge the necessity,
tasting salt.

Like a statue sits
this heart so hammered,
like a rock submerged, crushed under the fullness
of this surging pounding tide.
Oh rash one I! I invited herein the grinder
of spice in the pestle
to release that taste of the salt of the Earth
which apparently sings
Grinding bloody awful pain
it is.

How still is the rock
pounded and pressed by the surging sea
until the water runs out.
Throttle like a fruit.
Atlas carrying the sky.
The Thinker deep in gravity
pressed down.
Water runs out.
Squeeze blood from stones.
Strike the rock with hammer-blows,
Rod of Destiny,
this Soul tasting in essence
the salt,
the one who weeps knows not why, not where
it may ever end.

To taste the salt
is to retire into the depth of the blow
without protesting in surrender, being
there ever young,
ever open,
ever curious,
ever joyful,
for here is no time, and thus
no thought,
no pain,
there is the tasting of salt, the lake
welling water sharper than light
of life: blood, water, in the beating drink
Sorrow, drink Joy;
in the surfacing, form prison bars
from this voice to beat against. The eyes
are windows, pools of burning fire, red-rimmed,
silent spilling: when the high wave crashed on this house
timbers snapped and cracked as in the fire!
Wild white flame of water
silent, as in the grave.

There is such longing to embrace
thee, become safe.
Fools gold? turning to ashes? Love.
Yes, *that word, that knowledge.* Look and see.
The denial of love is a shuddering here.
The transmuting of love is a holy pilgrimage
among high mountains that the Sun enlightens.
Some attachment must then die to be born.
It must transcend the individual form.

The Place Of My Birth

I was not born in this land.
I was born beyond the distant water,
where eye cannot reach,
where only the eye of the heart can remember.
Sometimes I stand at the ocean's lapping brim
and try to recall how it was there
and how I came to this land.
What was the vessel that brought me here
and how long the journey?
I must have only been a stripling babe
when I arrived, ignorant of my origins
and I would have remained so
but for the gift of remembrance.
In remembrance will I reclaim the birthright
of my dawning day
and when I have done so
I will truly have returned home.

Within My Reach

The way out of
the mind's labyrinth
appears before me.

The last of the
coilings of the brain
is reached.

And suddenly
I find myself staring
out of its open mouth.

The mind's chatter
instantly ceases,

the eyes' endless
wanderings halt,

and immediately
there comes to me...

freedom...faith...joy...
peace and pure,
unbounded light...

and love
that is the heart
of life.

And all
within my reach.
Within my reach!

Sea Change

here
where the sky anchors clouds upon the sea,
where the rising tides lap the floor of heaven
and the ocean ebbs between the gates of the setting sun
here
float the weeds of memory,
their roots tangled in ancient wounds
still smarting from the sting of the moment,
weeds that congeal over the treasures below,
here
lie the years that have slipped beneath the surface,
memories sunk by the daily waves
needing the hook of tantalized taste buds
to draw up gems from childhood, vulnerable
to the astonished eye,
here
is determination to plunge
through alien water on locked lungs
evading the shadowing mouths to uncover
the encrusted shells of innocence,
prising open dead days
reaching for the pearl,
here
the sea's obtuse selection
of scuttled pain has scattered monsters
into the depths! let sunken traps
lie, no leviathans are challenged,
no Medusa heads need to be faced,
this perilous journey among barnacled tombstones
is to salvage heaven from the seabed,
here
where the sea glides into the star vault,
where the risk of midnight drowning is accepted,
courage can evoke angels from fallen days
for blessings here.

Queen Of The Arbour

A deepest darkling crimson August rose
So sweet, exhales her subtle mystic scent
Silently giving, equal to all; she knows
Whomever holds her stem of jade is heaven sent
To sip her precious wine of love and bliss.
He who fashioned such a fragrant sacred flower
Blesses the touch with a velvet petalled kiss
Before the sense savours the incense of the bower.

Happily in the Heart grows the rose of joy
Wafting waves of praise to her Friend above
Who formed the beauty of this bloom never to cloy.
The perfume of the rose transformed, returned as Love.

In such dusky Eden in an emerald dale
I did first hear the pining of the nightingale.

Light And Shadow

Even light has its darker underside.
Does not reason cleave meaning from meaning,
casting shadows of doubt?
Does not the tongue that darts ceaselessly
to separate truth from falsity ultimately become forked,
for is not the serpent the wise deceiver?

The sun knows no shadows.
It knows only the reality
of its own self-luminosity
and shines ever with the one light.

The Light

There is a Light beyond the darkness
Just as morning follows night
With an unexpected starkness
Shining beautiful and bright.
It is a Light you hope to find
In the midst of your despair.
Yet, hidden deep within your mind,
It is already there.
For through your tragic loss and pain
There's a choice that you must make
Between a newfound strength and gain
Or a heart that's sure to break.
You can decide that you will never trust
In the world or God again
And build a wall that you think must
Protect you from all men.
Or you can allow your tears to melt
That wall around your heart,
Unfolding motives never felt
Which will set you far apart.
For new depth and sensitivity
Will show themselves in you
As the sadness that you've had to see
Gives you something good and new.
And that Light, once so elusive,
Is no longer hid from view
But surrounds the world inclusive
As it radiates from you...

Unseen Brothers And Sisters

Lo, how we seem to dream each other's dreams
And recognise the source of all our songs,
Thus filling the coldest night with kinship.
Poor pilgrims we, to the Royal City,
Exiled children remembering their Home
Beyond the golden gates of the mystic dawn:
Secret Sun within the jewelled circle,
Radiant crystal, centre-set and pure.
O let us harmonise our better selves
And gently hold each precious kindly thought
Until that Love which is our heritage
Doth flow unseen from the sacred within
To inundate the arid lives of all.

What I Have Seen

What I have seen of God's face,
I cannot show you.

I can only scribble
indefinable outlines with dust,

a charcoal chiaroscuro
sketch for you, colourless.

But see how my hand moves.
Do you see dancing?

Time All Reckoning Exceeds

Time ne'er was told in minutes, hours and days
Nor sun, nor moon and stars will sing her praise
For she has silver wings to soar and float and fly
And reaches every margin of th'embroidered sky.

When flooding forth upon the drowned land
Her course will ne'er be stayed by human hand
In winding coils she dallies o'er the lea
Then spends herself in silence at the sea.

Time ne'er was bound in clanking clockwork toys
A reeking metal prison for our joys
For she has eyes to glean the smallest part
That veils the inner vision of the heart.

Spring

What vision of beauty is the spring,
Her dress the silver mists that swirl
O'er emerald hills,
Her voice the chaffinch that calls
Full-throated through the woods,
Her mood the stream that dances softly
O'er time-worn stones,
Her spontaneity captured in the laughing wind
That lifts the leaves in joyous gusts,
Tossing the buttercups' golden curls.

Mysteries

Deeper and further
And further and deeper,
As into enchanted
And fabulous seas --

What better and sweeter
Has ever been granted
Than after long fasting
Such banquets as these?

The prayers of all women
Condensed and distilled in
One magnified potion of power --
Aeons of brimming
Existence fulfilled in
The scope of one fathomless hour --

This well of abundance
That changes and blesses,
This flame that transfigures --
What tongue can frame this
That is better and higher than all earth possesses,
No letter nor symbol terrestrial expresses
This nameless
Ineffable bliss.

Pala d'Oro

Gold beaten smooth,
Gold embossed,
Gold sculpted,
Gold bejewelled,
Gold encased in geometry,
Your hymn resounds in glory.
Christ sits on his jewelled throne,
Its arms of pearls and garnet;
His book is of amethysts,
He raises His golden hand in blessing,
And jewels gleam in his halo
And in the hangings all around.
Row upon row of saints, prophets and angels,
Scenes of the Bible unfold,
And jewels to arrest the astonished gaze.
The human heart needs beauty to feed it,
To raise its sights above the earth.

Above, the prophets circle in the gold cupola;
The fierce eagle and the doleful bull look down,
Curve follows curve about the vaulted ceiling,
And shifting sunlight wakes up each in turn.

Emergence

Earth energies forcing growth
from darkness into light
Sun energies drawing form and colour
into Spring's new life

Inner energies rising and falling -
joyful crests, empty troughs
Alternating with Nature's patterns
of gold or grey

Time of awakening heart-flower
opening in life-love
Time of tears and stirring
deeply soul-stretched

Reaching upward, yearning for
the sun
With heartfelt longing -
Urge to grow and be

Inner promise, beginnings manifesting
on waiting Earth
Ready to nourish
her newborn child.

The Bow Of God

God's colours arch in the balance.

A downpour of fierce white hail in May
succumbs to a burst of sun

and a bright dome of seven colours
announces the equilibrium magically.

Rain is now pattering leaves and stones;
only the left spear of beauty retains its intangible brightness.

As the balancing colours of warmth, growth and spirit
melt back into the unknown realms,

I wish for this rainbow to fill the gap
where your sorrow and your joy battle.

Devotion

So submit child to God's almighty will
Understand his work shall anyhow be done.
Remember, if you wish to mount His holy hill
Regret no pain from past beneath the sun,
Eternally affirm all actions of the sacred One.
Now know 'I Am God' and then stay still
Denying nothing, drain thy cup and then refill.
Ever happy, tread freely, quietly fearing none.
Rejoice! for now thy arduous struggle has been won.

Silence

Some things remain unsaid,
Some things remain unheard,
The unsayable
Unspoken word,
Of love,
Of life,
Of living,
And
Sometimes
Of forgiving.

Nature Divine

All nature's mountains are monuments of Love;
all glad birdsong, a Marriage bell;
all nature's fruits, feasting for a Wedding night;
all sky's thunder, a Passion spell.

Love fires and infuses nature wholly, why?
Nature is God's body brought nigh.

Summer Awakening

One summer's day, full long ago, it came to pass
That earth and sea and sky - and all that therein was,
Did melt away in slow oblivion.
Withal it seemed that nature's blood entire,
Through but one vein did in abundance flow,
While the very being of the Universe
Was moved and quickened by a single pulse.
'Twas at that time I lost identity.
No more was I; I could have been a leaf;
A branch upon a tree - or yet a bird;
The sap of things - a breath upon the wind.
For one brief moment, nothingness was I.
Instead there came an all-pervading joy
Which silence has lingered till the present day.

The Soul's Desire

The flower desires the sun
By day, by night the moth the flame.
All things desire eternally,
The soul's desire is harmony:
Two notes that strike as one
And soaring suddenly blend
Will seem to swell a thousandfold
In widening waves of sound to send
A thrill of poignant joy through all the frame.

Snowflake

snowflake
mystery in white
miraculous creation
a blanket dream in miniature

artist
sculpting countryside
surprisingly wonderful
a perfect act of simplicity

magician
making memories
marvellously youthful
a perfect picture palace

season
silently serene
winter in idyllic form
a calendar of favourite moments

saviour
toboggan's ally
temptation's pure indulgence
a snowball's sense of happiness

Enchantment

The conjurer, the early morning sun
Struck crystal laden leaves with slanting light
And changed transparent monochrome
To shimmering waves of jewelled ice.

Emerald, topaz, sapphire
Enticingly gleaming, sparkling,
From nature's hoard of treasure
Unlocked for me this winter morning.

With childlike gaze of wonder
I observe this fleeting gift
Bestowed on humble mountain pasture,
Now a glittering carpet for my feet.

No trembling breath of frosted air
Nor the whisper of a sound
Violated the fragile, splendrous flair
Of a million gem stones scattered round.

Was I the only honoured guest
Of that matchless icy dawn
Perceiver of her phantom wealth
Entrusted briefly then, quietly gone.

New Age Wedding

The risen lark pours out its liquid hymn,
Calling footworn pilgrims to the Dawn.
The fire-crowned cockerel breaks the night,
And strikes the heart of sleep with dim-remembered fear.
Rejoice, O happy band of wedding guests,
Embrace your kith and kin of light and life,
Congregate in love, send forth hallelujahs,
For the Morning dons her flame feathered cloak
To greet the Sun enrobed in majesty and power.

Hail Babylonian, plotting on your inner chart
The burning path of Shamash, your King of Light.
Greetings, purest fire priests of Persia,
Kindlers of the heart's own holy flame,
Servers of the mighty throne of Mazda.
And Brahman, mediator of the morning,
Smearing thy lustrous face with butter,
And opening the golden eye of Self
To the living chariot of the Sun.
Druid, secretive yet radiant browed,
And wise in the mystery laws of Love,
Gathering spiritual fruits and flowers
As the first rays of the summer Day star
Penetrate deep within the forests of your mind.
And you Delphic archers, slayers of Death,
Lighting your torches at the blazing wheel of Day,
Shaking the dew from your fair locks
As Phoebus, the Prophetic, the Brilliant,
Rises to flood the mountain tops with waves of light.

Royal Priests of Egypt, greatest of the great!
Builders in the Spirit, renewing Now,
The solar flame of unpolluted Truth;
Beholding the morning boat of Ra
Proceed in radiant peace and glittering splendour
Across the turquoise ocean of the sky;

Minds raised to the dazzling Palace of the Sun,
From where His rays descend to waking Earth
Like stairways for the Salvation of his seed.

Where, O happy band, have the ages gone?
Since last we gathered here for the Dawn.
Where now the whirlwind, and where now the storm?
As we follow this procession of perfect Peace
To the Tabernacle of the Lord.

Dawn

At night it is as if Nature
holds her breath and
in the morning
releases it with a sigh
An ice-green-diamond dawn
Punctuated by
the Morning Star.

Parnassus

Why should I not dwell on fair Mount Parnassus,
home of my secretive Muse?
I know the labyrinthine cavern wherein she dwells
and attend her presence, patiently, at the entrance
many a long hour.
Sadly, she is not a creature of the sun-beam
and refreshing rain-shower:
but she responds to my voice when I sing to her
of how things were in days long ago
or read her some half-fogotten lay.
Once I have heard her first stirrings in the cavernous depths
she always appears to me suddenly,
lifting the veil from her face from time to time
and smiling sweetly.
When she speaks it is not to me:
rather, her lustrous voice plays through me.
Sitting at her feet I could listen to her revelations for hours
but beyond a certain point she turns her back on me
and returns silently to the darkness which is her home.
Now, in order to see her again, I must wait patiently.
As I wait, often my gaze falls on the plain,
where the cities lie:
how beautiful their white walls gleaming in the sunshine!
but I know what I cannot see: their dark hearts.
In such places there is a darkness
within which my Muse cannot dwell,
which is why she fled to fair mount Parnassus.

City life never was for me:
I prefer to sit where I can see!

Birthday

When the sting
of world's fragmented construct is drawn
from a wound, joy wells from the deep.

Like a rose whose opening
is clear water in dark brown pools,
a spring crystal bright in the dawn
drowns my darkness in delight.

To let this happen is to let it be.
So in slow subtle quietude unfurls
this flowering Source with thee,
in cool compassionate glance of our Lord,
as dew of light to drench the field.

As rain rises from deep deep down under,
through lush stems of radiant grass to tread;
as sparkling gems of sunlight splash
salt sea over open leaves of ancient rock
to the caress of pilgrim's palm and sole;
as song of the long dead, awakening,

so my eye of the heart
to you is open.
Your eye of the heart is a key
which entering this casket is free
for our intimacy beyond speech.
Ask it; I am given,
in the silence, yours.

In alarm, my small lunar steward,
fabric of thorns, of pageants
of noble and furtive wounds, so seekingly
striding about in broad daylight,
would rather hide from your sight.

Gently dismembering the hedge of phantoms
you enter the unbound glow of my Sun,
wherein to abide and breathe beyond speech.
This hidden chamber for you,
my Companion in the Light,
I find is pure and unashamed.

Once, during storm I saw a cicatrice thickly grown
up a tree which Nature split apart;
silent she cried out, her boughs spread wide.
I christened her my Isis-Tree,
Seeing in her openly, my history.

Dark cavern was in the breast and womb of Isis
lightening struck, grief stricken, Osiris needing.
You have entered, it seems, some place
which is beyond the bleeding,
by the grace of our Lord, with light.

You are present in this illumined peace
beyond measure, of the Sun
in the Sage's lamp which, morning fresh
and mourning free doth cleanse and deliver
in our mouth of Thoth, betrothal, I to I.

Here is infinitely undifferent the Eye.
Here, two halves of a seed divining
our Tree of Life at the root,
are sung within branches and boughs -
our tasks in life with those we love -
as Synthesis of Light,
Sefiroth in the stem.

In the Great Sage, our Lord,
such blendings are of small and kind account
in the merciful dark ocean of His eyes
which deftly guide the gardener

to uproot from dark soil the weeds
which painfully cling to appearance.

It abides
in an opening rose to sing,
of forbearance;

it reveals
in the thorn lifted out, the sting
of the world fragmented,

it lets
the current of the body healing
flow around the Rock of Ages, as in a mountain.

Angels

Poets weave a nest of golden fire
with their words
- a crucible to hold the heart,
whose language,
is the resonance in every atom,
in every molecule;

And in our weaving
we become what we are
- angels of the future.

Cooling Bluebells

When in the garden thunder rumbles low
And branches drip from early morning rain,
The bluebells' welcome coolness seems to glow
With primal colours in a charmed domain.

Against dark foliage deep amidst the shade
The bluebells sing an elegiac song -
Intensest blues our restless minds invade
And in our hearts refreshing chords prolong.

When dappled sunlight plays upon the flowers,
Their rainy surface glistens, fresh and new;
Blue, pink and white each draw on different powers
As swaying bluebells calming ploys pursue.

Their leaves, caressed by rain, proclaim fresh hope
And lift us outside petty human cares;
The garden's stirrings offer untold scope
For new perspectives which the year prepares.

Laburnum's golden racemes shower free
And mix with apple-blossom's frail display;
And orchard's petalled carpet is the key
To fruits which in due time will come our way.

Refreshed by early May's brief showers and sun,
And cheered by Spring's soft colours all around,
We hope to see the process here begun
By growth and ripe fulfilment later crowned.

A Winter's Mystery

A beech row windbreak
is masted in mystery
and frozen in the tall march
that climbs up the rise.

A sunrise of shooting light
catches the golden hues
as it scatters the darkness
in long shadow lines.

A crispness of breathing air
clings to the startled lungs
as a reminder of death
in a sharp frosted life.

A calmness in captured thought
crushes the nightmare fears
as a promise of wonder
catches beauty in bliss.

Final Awakening

Oh, sacred Fire-Self of all Supreme,
Ever eternal; unchanging Quality,
I thy happy beam in Water's teaching time
Am dreaming deeply in this changing flood;
My forms in joy and suffering, come and go,
Thy Essence reflected in the seven-fold Deep.

Dionysically, I as many represented,
This one half-fragmented to know its Self.
And now I touch with clinging dust
The clinging dust of Sleep;
Infinite extension in the Deeps of Time...
Oh, Awaken all ye dreamers!

Once pure Angel beyond all Time,
(Though mindless of Eternal Self)
Purity and Bliss your Quality,
Until projected into layers of substance,
Fragmented Self seemed lost
And dreamed the dream of reality.

Oh, Thou! one half dis-membered in the seeming...
As the heavenly Dolphin bursts from out moving Waters
Re-member your Self from the Cycles of Time!

Behold! a Single Star with Triple Aspect
Awakens upon the unabandoned Lotus.
Still unchanging Essence.
Yet now - a God of Conscious Fire;
Alive with fiery Understanding,
Unfolding undreamed of Riches
And wielding Powers of True Creation.
Full of keen, electric Life in Light;
In perpetual motion; undecaying,

Then two halves fused with unutterable Love,
Ascending as One to the Fire-Self Supreme,
To finally blend in Marriage Alchemic...
Eternal White Stone in the Mind of God!

Blue

In the dance of early morning there is harmony.
A Jay flows swiftly through the sky
to meet the softness of a butterfly.

In the ocean fish flash up from the deeps.
The radiance of their scales
are reflected in the eyes of a dancer.

He is dancing his beauty - his freedom.
The pattern is peace.

He sends his offering out
to the mist of all horizons
...to a glacier which sings its song.

Somewhere, somewhere a blind man
hears the song, feels the dance
- steps free from his inner darkness
and rises to meet the day.

Satchitananda

Dawn comes as a silent condor,
Breaking through remote recesses of the mind,
Like molten honey upon a sea of dreams.

The tide ebbs with the fading years,
Leaving footprints on the sands of memory,
Strewn with the beauty of coy, deserted shells.

The rippled pattern of the shore
Is but etched in rhythmic transient traces.
For life is a whisper of the universe.

In the light of love eternal,
The changing faces of man are illusion
For all is as nothing in timeless motion.

Gone is the glimpse of tomorrow.
There is only today forever dawning
And bliss in fulfilment of self-forgetting.

The Awakening

Returned once more, as if revived from death,
I stir from out the hidden depths of shade
To snatch again at that elusive flame.
So near at times, although it seems so far.
But now beyond my reach it slowly fades
As does that music dancing on my ear.

The Awakening Elements

Rejoice!
For dewy Earth doth stir from deepest sleep
And the scents of tinctured May float heavenwards
From all around her gentle form
To blend with bliss and joyfulness
Within the hallowed gardens of the Sun.
And drought is banished from her blighted land
As ancient springs pour forth their splashing life
To brim the mystic cup of self
With sacred draughts of Revelation,
Saving the lives of thirsty men
Who, like flaming nucleii of love, combine
In living constellations, bright and all ablaze,
Yet peaceful as the starlit night
Through which we pilgrims tread towards the Dawn
To gaze in wonder at the Symbol of our Lord.
And when distant kin reach out to touch our souls
From behind the veil of material life;
Or when healing airs that usher in the Day
Gently stroke our care-worn brows
And out of calmness, Self is born;
Then will pilgrims sing the songs of inner birth
And fill the holy ether with their hymns
And swoon amid the music of the spirit,
Chants of harmony which rise like incense
To the Glory of the One.

Simplicity

For those who know, there is no need to ask.
Asking disturbs the wayward intellect
And intellect is poison to the soul.
Be as a little child, of knowledge small,
Measured against the wealth of facts absorbed
By those who deem to know the universe,
Glib of theory, and quick to fashion laws.
And yet a little child knows more than they,
Walking the sunlit paths of innocence,
Still uncorrupted by vain thoughts of man,
Pure in the senses needed to translate
The riddle of the vast eternal plan.

There are no static laws to formulate.
The scene adapts, reforming much at will;
And ready interaction will dictate
What fluctuates, or wanders, or is still.
For there is no beginning and no end.
There is no minor self; no minor 'I';
Only the timeless, spaceless, ever One,
Intangible - elusive to descry.
There is no birth or death; we come and go
Like scudding clouds across a summer sky,
And yet, in splendour, form again elsewhere,
Without a need to know the reason why.

There is no need to verify the truth;
No need for confirmation or for proof.
Savour each precious moment most tenderly;
Rely on mystic sense - not what you see.
And in due course, out of tranquillity,
Born of a quiet nothingness, will come
A feeling of absorbed simplicity,
And consciousness that everything is One.

Eternity Of Now

On a summer's day
When I was walking alone
In the countryside
It seemed earth and sea and sky
Vanished and just I remained

And it seemed to me
That all Creation's being
Quickened to one pulse
And all of Nature's life-blood
Flowed within the heart of me

And I was not I
But a tiny bright green leaf
A tree or a bird
A soft breeze bending the grass
Or the life in all these things

For one brief moment
I was total nothingness
And yet everything
And in that moment I found
The eternity of now

Golden Threads

But we are the distant voices
That call from river and sea,
From subterranean cavern
And windswept mountain peak;
From ice-bound polar region
And dreary wastes of sand,
From the sombre depths of ocean
And the brilliant skies of day.

For we are painters of visions,
The creators of movement and light,
Of the fantasies and vistas
That illuminate the mind.
But we are also builders of legends,
Of the mysteries, marvels and myths
That appear with the dawn of perception,
With the birth of original thought.

We dance within the rainbow,
Our inscriptions line the clouds;
They decorate each sunbeam
And they glow when daylight fails.
For we are the cosmic conscience,
And we weave the fabric of life -
With silver strands of starlight
And golden threads of hope.

Reverie

Oh let me in sweetest peace and treasure dreams
Lay me down gently upon the dew-spangled moss,
When the soft flames of stars enchant the Night
And silvery elves in graceful circles dance.
Then, memories like soft murmurs move me deeply
Into far distant Realms of the long ago,
And I, like a Spark of Fire into the Night,
Leave the wingless Earth sleeping far beneath me,
And enter the Innocence of Beauty and Light.

Lover And Sufi

This be the goal of your zeal --
This be the whole of your zeal --
With every song reveal --
With every breath attest --
That the ultimate vision of Love's ideal
But waits for two wills to become the real,
Living and manifest.

For the heart is a mirror
And, as we draw nearer,
The image within it grows steadily clearer,
Till we
Shall be
Aware
That the flawless reflection of Love's perfection
Exists embodied there.

Summer Bridesong

In bejewelled splendour
with colours ablaze
Earth's heart fast beats
Her beauty shines
through blossoms
reflecting rainbow hues,
cradled in a sea
of green richness.

She trembles
as a blushing bride
awaiting her beloved
and all life sings
her love song
of open surrender
as radiant now
she lies with
warm and scented breath.

The Ring-Dove

One with the equilibrium of nature
insensible of my own delight
I stood
moments like years
and might never have woken
save that the ring-dove clapped -
and the spell was broken!

In The City Of The Heart

In the City of the Heart,
Love is the mortar
that binds every stone.
And there is no divide.

In the City of the Heart,
rivers of compassion
flow in every street.
And there is no divide.

In the City of the Heart,
the light of beauty
garlands every creature.
And there is no divide.

In the City of the Heart,
flowers of humility
bow down in prayer.
And there is no divide.

In the City of the Heart,
the perfume of devotion
fills the air.
And there is no divide.

The City of the Heart
lies between the space
between each heart-beat.
And there is no divide.

In the City of the Heart,
all who enter
are made whole again.
And there is no divide.

Golden Dawn

The centred circle
Shines out bright

Beauty born
In a barren world

Gold shimmers
Flooding light

Orb of love
Open my heart

Golden dawn
Bathe this fawn

Melt the night
Into memory.

The Traveller

When senses hang as heavy curtains
eyes nor mind can acknowledge
the luminosity of human spirit;
the petal-soft lustre, the flame, the fire.

The logic-torn mind, the intellect
burdened with unsung songs
disowns the soul, the waterfall
cascading stillness from hidden
crevices in rocks.

Having seen no rainbow in droplets;
having heard no symphony of heart, mind;
leaving echoes trapped in stone of silence
the traveller moves on.

Friendship

You shared, dear friends with me and mine,
The broken bread, the blood red wine.
And by this sacrament divine,
The sacred oaths of friendship made.

And thus distinguished, thus defined,
Our fellowship was fast enshrined,
In bonds that stand the rape of time,
And fondness that shall never fade.

Monologue

Who would remove the crown of thorns?
Who would carry the cross?
Whose body, whose blood, whose heart?
Who's forsaken, torn apart?

Stars burst, planets collide.
World's always falling apart.
Grounds quake, shake, sink.
Storms rage all night.

Loss, pain, fear, doubt.
Ghosts in closets, shadows abound.
Merely labels, designed by mind.
Own creation, own find.

Watching present, dissolve in past.
Blaming triggers, slipped emotions.
Couldn't past be kernel of present?
Couldn't flowers bloom in ashes?

However, far the echo, faint the murmur,
Waves in waves of consciousness.
Tune in, the rhythm of life.
Blend in, the Immanence sublime.

On the slippery slope of time,
As washed pebble, hold your head high.
Sing to waves, dance with tides.
Reclaim your sparkle, your heart.

Five Little Gems

There's a glorious garden on my Island of Gold,
Casting spears of enlightenment *through* my Tree,
Bedecked with bright Flowers and Mystical Gems,
Awakening the true I while transmuting me!

Why should I weep when fettered by me?
Am I not brooding on my own selfish sea?
Though I *seem* a sad captive in this dark earthy Cave,
From beyond me I observe me alive in this Grave!

I was once lost in my deep filthy mire,
Till my lower self melted in Love's secret Fire.
Now pure bells ring sweetly from my Magical Tree,
Ringing sweet joyful Love Gems *through* I unto thee.

I dare you surrender in Peace to the Flame;
To give up your baubles for the One without name.
I dare you to Trust in the Secret Light Plan;
Amidst the dark animals ... dare to be Man!

How could You be snared by their sugary bribes,
When all is dissolving in a seven-fold Fire Law?
Or chased by the hounds of your mean selfish fears,
When vast awesome Mysteries knock at your Door?

Cosmic Vision

Imagine a tapestry of precious stones,
Diamond, topaz, ruby, tourmaline,
Sapphire, emerald, all cluster in between,
Ornamenting heaven with their rainbow tones.

134

Each reflected lustre each appears to own,
In harmony from galaxy to gene,
Inter-related, an ethereal scene
Enjoyed by Consciousness, One and all alone.

Uncaused, spontaneous, without an end,
Infinite jewels arise; gems of dust
Illuminated, mirroring as they must
The dance of cosmic music God did send.

All things dissolving to no Thing at all
Rhythms of the spheres pulsate and fall.

Colourflow

The woman stepped lightly on scented clouds
Rising to the sky temple
And opening the wide and welcoming doors
Entered a chamber of treasures.

There, in the centre, stood a tree of flowing gold
And hanging from its branches living jewels
In the magic way she ate the gems
Then breathed upon sleeping humanity
Streams of purest colour.

When they awakened and their sight was clear
They saw their planet truly
They looked upon her beauty - from their hearts
And wept.

The Painter

With each stroke of the brush,
At each glance,
A new horizon
Is within my sight.

As the light from a clear sky,
Pierces the stream,
Then rises like a diamond,
And floats from my view,
I am captured
Upon the surface of the water.

As the canvas
Becomes more complete,
As more power,
More knowledge,
More understanding,
Continues to colour my world,
The painter shows a genius,
I can no longer ignore.

In these valleys and glens,
Beside rivers and streams,
Below snow capped mountains,
Where eagles caress the air,
I have walked with the wise man,
The master of serene beauty,
The musician of my soul,
The prince of light,
The painter of colours,
Upon the canvas of life.

Hymeneal

The warm air was tranquil and rich with perfume,
Drifting up from the bushes below us in bloom.
She stood at the railing, her head on her hand,
And her eyes on the slow-setting moon.

I looked at the stillness and peace on her face.
Then I too turned my eyes to the night.
And together we followed downwards through space
The moon with its halo of white,
Trailing behind the obscurely massed black
Of the bushes and foliage its luminous track;
Till the last pallid ray had been carried away,
And the stars shown more piercingly bright.

As I gazed at that sky I remembered
How under that limitless height
I had turned in despair from the emptiness there
And averted my face at the sight.
That sky now so flowing with splendours past knowing,
So tender, so laden with light!
And there welled from within me a thanksgiving hymn,
That went up with our love through the night.

I encircled her waist, she turned slowly,
Her eyes were veiled over and dim,
She swayed as I gathered her closer,
Like a reed that is bent by the wind.
Then her half-open mouth had met with mine,
And all that had happened before that time
I no longer remembered, and all I had done,
And all that I was, or might yet become,
And all I had ever been.

I walk homewards slowly, my being
Athrob with the thrill of her kiss,

And look round me in wonder at seeing
A changed world through the veil of my bliss,
And walk and without knowing where.
I cross through a square and am not aware,
Voices call to me, I do not hear.

I speak to the trees, to the flowers, to the breeze,
To the birds overhead sailing by,
Sing, laugh and cry,
Then, without knowing why,
Sinking down on my knees, underneath the sky
Pour blessings on everything living,
With praises and tears of thanksgiving.

Rainfire

Like bright gems the raindrops hang
from a twig
Pear-shaped jewels flashing
rainbow fire
As they are pierced by
a shaft of sunlight.

A Song Of Unity

I AM FULL as a mountain lake after summer rain
That's fed the stream and source of wisdom, love;
A fire sent by God to ignite his planet, from above,
The golden glow of heat on burnished plain
Gilding every leaf on this pilgrimage in lover's lane,
Warming Earth, her gritty ochre clay.
Water, sea of mercy, green and grey.
Air, the breath of life so free from pain
Crystalline, beyond the play of loss or gain.
What does it mean to my Master, white as turtle dove?
This vast empty void, an abyss, a lonely way
Of trial; the costly pearl that pilgrim has to pay.

What of scripture, tracts, gospels and sacred books,
The Lord's lurid library of command and revelation?
A crore of scribbling, comment with endless emendation,
These holy tomes which cram cathedral nooks and crooks
To surfeit, and provide much cawing, as a score of rooks.
Is this Self-knowledge, Upanishadic or Socratic?
Or pathology of mind, narcissistic, autocratic?
Even freed, by wisdom and the Sage, from senses, it looks
A hotch-potch well prepared by the devil's favourite cooks
To titillate the palate to a novel sensation.
So what is freedom from desire vulgarised by folk-democratic?
But my Master who is One, without a second, is truly aristocratic!

What is knowledge of Truth, Self Realisation, Enlightenment.
Or ignorance, sleep, alienation, dark delusion
Or folly dithering in the dream of world illusion?
Or freedom from bondage, desire, and slave attachment?
What is the meaning of these questions, the prime predicament?
What is the deep significance of ego 'I thought', 'I conceit'
Mistakenly wed to body-mind, to bed in self-deceit?
What is this 'mine', a grabbing hand, a grasping temperament
For many objects, trinkets, attractive and so vehement?
Or the form of Self Consciousness, to save me from confusion?

To rescue Soul from duality and its preordained defeat.
So I pray for Grace and mercy at my Master's sacred feet.

I am That, Absolute, unique, always One
As consciousness, love, awareness, bliss,
Embraced by the love of God, blest by his kiss;
In the light of glad glory, radiant as the Sun
I am always homogeneous, second then to none.
What care I for freedom from charnel chains or liberation
In life or death, or the game of gaining Realisation?
Or for my current worldly destiny predisposed to run
Rebirthing in an alien womb 'till kingdom come?
And after transmigration, at-one-ment I may miss.
My Master stops this baffling mental masturbation...
I let go, unknowing, abiding in the Heart of silent adoration.

I have no central 'I-notion' resident at home,
There's no one to be elated or badly hurt by fear,
Pleased, perplexed, pouting, proud, or simply here
To feel depressed, anxious; a mind to roam
Over an inward seascape of bubbles, froth and foam.
So where is he who suffers, enjoys and acts,
Who has strong opinions and knows *all* facts?
What is the rising or vanishing of thought beneath the cerebral dome,
What is this visible world? the bauble of an impish gnome?
So here and now there's no fictional person to jeer or leer,
For my Master the cards are neatly dealt in stacks,
Abidance in Heart, in the Real Self, no need for lofty tracts.

So set in temple-shrine of the Spiritual Heart
Nestling on the dexter side of my heaving breast
Not on the left where the fleshy pump beats in my chest,
Dwells 'I-Amness' which awakening does start.
So pondering, I put the question, what is the part
I play on life's stage, and what is this world?
Who yearns for freedom from prison in which I'm hurled?
Oh, what is Oneness, awareness, Truth, and wisdom's art?
Into which was fired Love's rose flowered dart?

Who is bound or free as the honoured friend and guest
Behind the body-mind and now at last unfurled
As space for the Universal to happen in, lustrous and impearled?

So deep in my Spiritual Heart, I am the One, unborn,
Uncaused, deathless, new, eternal, free,
I enquire, what is this tempestuous, stormy, troubled sea
Where froth is foaming, bubbling from eve to morn
On the ocean of Self, fired by an Orient dawn?
So what is Creation, what means world-dissolution?
I ponder these questions and search for a heartfelt solution.
Who and what is seeking? A King, Bishop or pawn
On this splendid chequered emerald palace lawn?
What is the goal of searching, is it peace, freedom, liberty?
Who is the bold seeker to seek the final absolution,
And what has he found as the answer? The ultimate resolution!

I am pristine, pure as the driven Himalayan snow
As a pellucid stream pouring from pinnacle's height
Chaste, flawless, without blame, and wintry white.
I trickle down the mountain valley to the river and flow
Free! I am curious about what there is to know,
By what dubious method is knowledge gained
And what spurious end, when it is attained?
I have no problems either in heaven, here, or in hell below,
I have surmounted grief, elation, sorrow, born of woe,
Simply stated, I know what is meant by wrong and right,
This universe by creation, preservation, destruction, is maintained
By the Grace of God and His Almighty Will; all creatures are
                                        sustained.

Here, awakened now, I am steady, perfectly still
As an adamantine rock in the restless ocean stands
Unmoved by wind or wave or shifting sands.
What are the contrary oppositions sick, healthy, ill,
Pleasure, pain, to quickly heal or swiftly kill --
Distraction, concentration, contemplation, perturbation, meditation,
Reflection, rejection, abstraction, negation, confirmation? --
The Master transcends these, he welcomes all as God's Almighty Will.

He accepts what is, experiences all, as gracious grist to his mill.
Gently through Grace of God he breaks all bondages' bonds.
In a great paeon of praise in unconditional affirmation
He rests one with Totality, his Self -- a conscious consummation.

I have lost the monotonous merry go round of thought.
Perpetual treadmill of self-opinion and words,
Mainly cynicism, lies, like the flapping wings of birds,
A poisonous brew so often bitterly fraught
With the mistaken idea that I ought
To cherish the intellect, the mind is the Chief;
Am I to be robbed by thought, that villainous thief?
So that's the lesson my dear Master patiently brought:
Ignore these scorpion stings of concept with which you're wrought,
All this inner discussion is really absurd --
Here is consciousness, a gift beyond any belief!
This ending of thought brings peace, ultimate joy, relief.

I am clarity, pure as crystal, lily white
Growing in a purple thistle-bracken field.
So what is illusion? To this question I yield
For finite mind cannot understand the infinite
And magic of 'maya' is a brilliant trick of light.
What is this world, a dream, a notion, concept? It appears
As symphony deceiving even the soundest of ears.
An emptiness of 'I' conceit, a simple void like night
Is for witness. - Self, the nakedness of inward sight.
So here and now, what appears within the onion peeled?
The master wipes away my grief and all my tears.
All is well, unfolding as it should, to allay my foolish fears.

With no hint of Duality, One without two
Unity, Oneness, Unicity, Wholeness, Seamless,
All of a piece, consciousness, love, awareness
There's nothing to divide or separate me from you;
Divine perfection emanating from a primal source, who
Am I, but That? I am eternal, the same
Existence, Truth, God, without a Name.

Now I know there is nothing the 'me' can do;
All that is happening is God's Will, right through and through.
I rest in the Heart blissful, benign, blameless,
So what is my little Soul to the Almighty God of flame?
The Master says "unknown, unique, celebrate, enjoy His game!"

For endless striving and effort, where is the need?
Struggling against one's natural way and feeling
Trained from cradle to prevail, practising fair dealing,
Pressed to labour hard if you wish to barely feed
A family, own a home, a car, and so succeed,
Ingrained, conditioned as a machine well oiled,
Poor pilgrim's become half baked and partly boiled.
So my Master to his students does earnestly plead
Be still, be motiveless when you perform a deed,
So forget the books, the aims, the teaching and the kneeling,
After all the hard years you've zealously ploughed and toiled
Open wide, relax, uncoil, and never by the world be spoiled.

I have no limits, I am no longer bound --
No edges, marges, verges, remain for me.
Nothing arises. I am empty space for all to see
That all is well. My true Self I have found.
I traced my 'I thought' like a hunting hound
And discovered my primal source, the light of day,
And now as witnessing consciousness I'm free to play.
So I rest in my Heart near a sacred mound.
Where my naked feet tread is holy ground.
I've found freedom! joy, bliss and liberty.
No thing is, I am God. What more is there to say?
I've recognised the truth of Self, the non-dual Way!

Paean In Three Short Movements

Sun

Sun, I know you, though you would not know me
Among so many friends, but I am he
Who waits upon the shortest day
To catch your glances as crouching low
You reappear above the ridge tiles' filigree
And pass behind the gnarled fret of an old apple tree.
You make bleak gardens edible with snow,
And scour dark streets with lashing rain,
Fill sullen rivers up to overflow onto flat meadows
Then breathing out warm the chilled furrow of the weald,
And stitch the pleated drills with autumn grain;
Then breathing in draw up great draughts
Of sap, which make the orchards stretch and yawn.
And blink new fragile leaves
And open crowded blossoms row on row.
I see you brush green bracken on the russet moor
And pen brief swallows on a parchment sky.
The time to sow becomes a time to reap.
Mists gather early and are slow to clear,
The patient birch waits in stark elegance
To enter winter's chamber half asleep

Sun, you should know me. Swallows and I are kin
That should we fall from splendid flight, we cannot rise again
On our own wings. With you in arrogance and origin,
Being more heat than light
We make a god in our own image, envious
And so believe our downfall is sheer spite;
But with all things we disappear and reappear
Through the dark mirror of embracing night.

Sun, you do know me
For when at noon I walk within
The narrow shade of a wall
Tracing its courses with my finger tips
And hesitate before an open door,
It is your arm which draws me through
Into a place of water and a vine
To find a name unreadable upon a trodden stone,
To feel a child's hand too wise for words
Rest lightly upon mine,
Whose eyes, clearer than innocence,
Gaze into nowhere through my face in rapt content
And we are both together,
And alone.

Honey Eyes

Honey eyes bubble in your butter face
Spilt mirth flows down your apple cheeks.
Lips pause and sneak into a grin,
Smile pebbles ripple in your eye pools.
Joy crowns you like a wreath of haw flowers
You throw your head back and a haze
Of haw petals shimmer in a pale sun.
You lift your lids to glance my way,
A barnful of butterflies jitter in me.

Shadows Of Eternity

It now is twilight in this northern land,
When earth becomes mysterious and vague,
Its landmarks, contours, seeming to dissolve,
While day and night still struggle for control;
And I am sitting at a viewing point,
A cliffside terrace, high above the sea.
I am alone, a stillness now pervades
This element of our terrestrial sphere
Save that a rhythmic note comes from below -
The sound of breakers beating at the rocks.

The placid ocean is an inky black,
Though in the distance there are points of light
That glitter from the isles that dot the bay.
There also are those tiny sparks that change
Location and may sometimes disappear
As though they emanate from vehicles
That wind their way along those hidden roads
Around the fringes of the island shores.
The contours of the hillsides and the coasts
Are faintly outlined by a gentle glow.

But now I feel detached from time and space,
For looking at those dark'ning eastern skies
I find some twinkling gems have now appeared,
So that the air of mystery I sense
Extends until the cosmos is embraced.
While now that rhythmic movement seems to change
From waters lapping at our global shores
To one that swells throughout the universe,
Through which the flow of consciousness evolves -
And merges with the fields of endless time.

Orchard Fulfilment

Where Spring once lavished blossoms pink and white
To lift the wintry heart with pure delight
Then scattered petals in a graceful shower,
Firm fruit comes pushing on from fragile flower.

The orchard's magic soon has run its course
With vibrant Nature's rhythms out in force:
We watch the swelling fruit on laden trees
As wood is pumped with tireless energies.

This generous miracle returns each year,
A sign of God's involvement in our sphere:
Its providential regularity
Suggests a contant loving care to me.

Not that the harvest always is the same,
For mutual partnerships must be the aim,
And clearly we must play our proper role
As part of Nature's self-sustaining whole.

In due time we must prune and feed and spray
To bring the trees' potential into play;
Meanwhile these quiet orchards gratify
The birds who teach their nestlings how to fly.

At length ripe shades of yellow, red and green
Appear in plums' and apples' healthy sheen;
With daily tempting visions we are faced -
At proper time, how luscious to the taste!

What can compare with fruit that's freshly picked?
The grower's joy is hard to contradict
Whose happy teeth are privileged to sink
In juicy flesh so creamy or so pink!

So let's thank God for His creating fruits
With all their many healthy attributes:
Their sugar, fibre, vitamins and juice
And life-enhancing features they produce!

And people ripen, too, as years succeed
And grow more mellow both in word and deed;
We hope for full fruition, and we yearn
To see our dreams to brighter prospects turn.

Desert Bloom

Somewhere in that arid patch of earth,
life-force was dormant --- resting, waiting,
for a whisper, a breath, an awakening.
a wish to waken, a seed to ripen.

Sand grains --- infinite bits of broken
mirror reflected the secret longing
rooted in wish, moistened with yearning,
mirage turned miracle, desert bloomed.

Poised between creation and consciousness,
nestled among tender shoots, spiky leaves,
was desert bloom, rising from deathly slumber
into dewy freshness, colour, and light..

Garden Lover

Ours is a quiet passion
Not carried forward on the pulse of blood
But by insinuation of cool sap from cell to cell
Through the placenta of deep soil
Lifting an alphabet of ions
Into the teeming meristem
Which sets out laddered leaves
Enticing light and air
To conjure scented flowers and sugared fruit

When I reach in with saw and secateur
From my small conscious into your rich unconsciousness
I aim to take only what can be spared
And spare all that is needed to renew
Then I will through the summer laze
While you seduce with slow encroachment
On my green island lawn
Until the fall of leaves and briefest days
Urge me to prune again

I shall be pruned in my own winter quiet
Thus be subsumed into that fertile store
From which all gardens grow
And be returned to undergrowth and thicket
But should another gardener come
Then he will know there once was garden here
And reaching in with secateur and saw
Through patient year on year,
Reveal and then restore the old design
Conceding it is neither his nor mine.

The Inward Light

Why do you yearn to be in constant quest
When what you seek but lies without your door
Or fills the soul and always lies within?
So simple is the answer to your dreams -
So obvious - that it is unobserved.
Suffice to know that you have treasure now;
For rich perfection was on you bestowed
When you were fashioned first among the stars.
Brushed with the essence of immortal dust.

For thus formed long ago in mystic light,
The magic that was you was slowly breathed
Into a lowly cell for human birth;
And though your mind has limits of its own,
Which veil the concepts of your early source,
Before the dawn may come - though not at will -
In the Non-Space and Non-Time; lucid - still -
A glimpse of what was once...will always be...
A link, in rapture, with eternity.

Transition

The breath of a crystal cool wind
refreshes my impatient heart
purifying, cleansing it
of the debris of the past,
preparing a way
for the magpie collection
of experiences to come.

It creates a calm space,
a restful place
in which to wait on
the will of other time
For I do not live
in splendid isolation,
choosing when and where
I move,
but flow with the pattern
that unfolds without pause.

I pass through doors
marked 'Heart's Desire'
when openings are presented.
For therein lies my Truth -
and potential to be expressed
in form.
Therein lies my purpose -
and soul-growth
to be realised.

I strive to accept
the everturning wheel of Fate,
full knowing that
within the everpresent NOW
lie the seeds of
my future
and my destiny.

The Shrine Of The Moon Lady

Your presence was a place of peace,
Of rest from wandering, and sweet release
From weariness and pain.
I entered as into the sheltering shade
Of a fresh and flowering forest glade,
Yet moist with cooling rain.
A shadowy shrine, a tranquil retreat,
For one who comes in from the parching heat
Of a sun-baked noonday plain.
A circle of calm I found at your side,
A sanctuary sanctified,
And balm for heart and brain.

There exists a garden beneath a wall,
Where once I saw a moonbeam fall
Through the branches overhead.
And does it not seem that ray that shone
On those leaves in the night is yet my own,
And that could my steps be led
Back to that garden grove once more,
I should find that moonbeam as before,
Though the blossoms are shrivelled and dead.
-- I do not remember at all the rays
Of sunlight I have seen ablaze
On many and many a head.

Horizon

He fell asleep that afternoon
cradled in their conversation,
dreamed of sunlight, beauty,
death and transformation.

He travelled to the kingdom of the Shades
the still, sad music of humanity
a recurrent undertone
near the almost silent sea.

He did not shrink - the Stygian gloom,
dark, menacing, remorseless grey,
with the flood of Acheron
drove hope and joy away.

But not for long - lyrical, the
sweet petals of the cherry tree:
songs from the lexicon of love, he asked
Charon to read them and to set him free.

So in those close Elysian fields
he knew the joys of life again,
wind kissed the music and he woke
to a new and wonderful refrain.

From 'When These Times Are Gone'

Thy Mind shall rise unto the Light
And reborn anew shall become that Light
Stretching from the world
Unto the breathless beauty of Heaven.
Thus shall we joy together in the Beauty of God's Light.
And together with our beloved Kin, who even now await our return,
We shall walk amid the gentle flowers
That drink the rainbowed mists of paradise,
Or perhaps be borne away on soaring wings
And hidden within the Higher Mysteries of Illumination.
And so through me shall you find the Path
For I, I am the Way, whose time is soon and shall not be denied.
I, the steeply slanting Ray; I, the Gate that leads to Glory.
Come, ye pilgrims all,
Come thee to thy Lord of eternal Life in Light.
O may Destiny unfold
To shower thy Minds
With Light and Beauty and Love;
And may Necessity bring thee to the Safety
Of our Heavenly Home.
The forests once thick with the night
Shall smile emerald smiles beneath the beamy dawn,
And as the mists of the earth evaporate beneath the rising sun
So shall your dreams of unreality
Vanish in the consciousness of my Presence
And you shall rise above the place of aching hearts
To bathe thy mind in radiance,
Cleansing from it the stains of the world.
For I, I am the Mind of Light, whose time is soon and shall not be
                                                        denied,
I, who penetrate the barriers of the flesh
To bring illumination to those who are mine.
O may all creation lift up and rise
To blend in full Awareness with the Mind of God Almighty.
And may the grim acts of Man,
Heaped one upon another down through the ages,
Be washed away by the Benevolence of His Light.

Samadhi

Pulsing and moving; all things are changing,
In fond cascades of energy and light.
A fleeting moment serves but to transform
All that was once familiar to the sight.
All that perchance seemed lost becomes renewed,
For nothing dies; but flourishes again,
In incandescence, wondrous to behold;
Magnificent; but on a higher plane,
Where hues, unknown to artists heretofore,
Filter through many mansions undefined;
Where all is Love and Egos are no more,
And all are One - forever unconfined.

Acquiescence

My head pulsates as though I have become
An islet in a dark and boundless sea.
A sea of utter weariness and pain,
In which, though semiconsciously, I float
Devoid, of sense of purpose or a will.
Content, however aimlessly, to drift
Wherever drawn by current or by tide.
For I am now bereft of all desire,
Such as I may perhaps have once possessed,
For anything within the stream of life -
Save acquiescence to what now appears
Must be in fact a universal flow.

What does it matter how I reached this state?
I may have been ill-fated, out of luck,
Or else humility may have inspired
Those lessons that I truly know so well -
How best to take those blows that fortune deals,
Accepting all the problems that arise,
And not returning venom, drop for drop.
While all around are isles that likewise drift,
Though unaware that they may lack control,
That there will be a moment, unforeseen,
An instant that may still be undefined,
When they themselves must finally succumb.

But yet, despite the problems of this world,
I still can see the silent planets move
Against that background of the twinkling stars,
Themselves the emblems of a cosmic force,
That shine like signposts through the floods of time
To help Creation on its endless task -
Through which, unchecked, the mute millennia pour.
So that I feel, despite my own distress,
My apathy, and that unceasing strain,
The cosmos glows with purpose, end to end,
And stirs as though its mind is in accord -
With what it was that its Creator willed.

Maestro

The blackbird seems to know
The shape of the field of silence that expects his song.
Almost ironically he sings
To fill that mould.
That elemental force he puts on show
That passion drive and
Effortless prolixity
Merely point up
Reserves.
He leans back in the gaps
He lets us feel the leisure in his throat
The notes he chooses not to let us know.

.

In Harmony

In the silence of her eloquent smile
A realm of mighty fame is spread,
This scene of joy and wonder sparkles
Like stars upon the peaceful lake,
Forever we sail calm in our overflow of smiles,
Which like the bliss of light would come and go,
Such music in harmony with our tears caress,
The ecstacy on Earth to be so blessed.

Surviving all mortal change amid bolts of lasting loveliness
The moonlight lamps of Heaven shone,
Which gave us hope
Driving us on;
Steady yet swift, within this the flow of life,
Bright in the lustre of our new found joy
Exposed to the precious change - we smiled once more,
With echoed thoughts we share the charm
In unity eternally there.

Come Lord Of My Existence

Come, lord of my existence, who possess
The depths and flaming heights of paradise
With all its hundred levels and its light
And wait - - and still command
Patience and try my soul and have
All heaven in your hand - -
Come, lord of my existence, and require
Love only. Perfect. Passionate. Entire
Devotion. Nothing else and nothing less.

The Goal Of Love

Before the wonder of a soul laid bare
To feel a sense of worship so devout,
A certitude so absolute that there
Can be no possibility of doubt - -
The moving vision of a soul without
The veils that hung like stifling clouds between - -
And is this not the goal of love, the dream?

Beyond the shores of outwardness to see
A never-ending ocean stretch and know
How infinite a human soul can be,
Depth upon depth, as far as thought can go - -
To float untrammelled towards each other, flow
In woven currents, vanish and be whole - -
And is not this the dream, the end, the goal?

I Wonder What We Did

I wonder what we did when we were One.
Before our spirits entered body form.
Perhaps we wandered free in sylvan glades
And listened to the music of the dawn.
Ours would have been a purer, kinder love,
Untarnished yet by body or by mind;
There would have been no heartbreak and no pain
And no usurping ego laying claim.
For the mad passion I now feel for Thee,
Would have assumed a far more tender role;
Far more subdued in quiet reverence,
Calmed by the mystic beauty of your soul.

·

Happiness Mantra

All is well in healthful
heart
All is well in wealthful
world
All is well in infinite
future
All is well in finite
past
All is well within
me
All is well without
me
All is well
All is well
All is well.

Love Is!

Love is, expressible and creative
far deeper than the deepest well,
Love is, a spring, as it ripples and flows
into a fathomless ocean,
Love is, the sanctity of The Spirit
for it transcends the physical,
a candle of this World, soon extinguished!
Love is, the Child of Holy Innocence
eternal Spring of The God Head founded,
to its Divine source, returns!

INDEX